CHOOSING A FAITH

BRIEFINGS is a new series of short books to explain and clarify complex contemporary subjects, written for the non-specialist by experts in their fields. Themes and topics covered will include Feminism, Education, Cosmology, Medical Ethics, Political Ideology, Structuralism, Quantum Physics and Comparative Religion among others.

CHOOSING A FAITH

Ninian Smart

BRIEFINGS
Series Editor: Peter Collins

BOYARS/BOWERDEAN
LONDON. NEW YORK

First published in 1995 jointly by
the Bowerdean Publishing Co. Ltd., 8 Abbotstone Rd, London SW15 1QR
and Marion Boyars Publishers, 24 Lacy Rd., London SW15 1NL
and 237 East 39th St., New York, NY 10016

Distributed in Australia and New Zealand by
Peribo Pty Ltd, Terrey Hills, NSW 2084

British Library Cataloguing in Publication Data

Smart, Ninian
  Choosing a Faith. – (Briefings Series)
  I. Title II. Series
  291

Library of Congress Cataloging-in-Publication Data

Smart, Ninian, 1927–
  Choosing a faith / Ninian Smart.
      p.   cm. — (Briefings)
  1. Religions. 2. Faith. I. Title. II. Series: Briefings
(London, England)
  BL80. 2. S594   1995
  291 —dc20   94-31505
                                                  CIP

ISBN 0 -7145 -2982- 6 Original Paperback

Designed and typeset by Bowerdean Publishing Co. Ltd.
Printed and bound in Great Britain by Itchen Printers Ltd., Southampton.

CONTENTS

Chapter 1   Choosing and Judging Worldviews   1

Chapter 2   A Map of the World's Religions   22

Chapter 3   How Religions May Agree   42

Chapter 4   Judging Ideas and Teachers   62

Chapter 5   By Their Moral and Social Fruits   86

Chapter 6   Judging Worldviews in the Global
              World   99

              Bibliography   108

              Index   109

CHAPTER ONE

CHOOSING AND JUDGING WORLDVIEWS

W e live in a world of choice. That is, we who read books like this. Maybe a poor farmer in Bangladesh has few choices, and might find the idea of choosing a faith ridiculous. But we who are well beyond subsistence live in a world which is global, plural and consumer-oriented. Increasingly it is democratic and individualistic. Because the world is global all faiths and value-systems come to meet together. In Bombay and London, Los Angeles and Bangkok, Milan and Moscow, there are men and women of different religions and cultural outlooks living together. And even if they were not living side by side they would be seeing one another through the media. Now, in a society which is highly homogeneous, people do not meet other value-systems. They take their worldview for granted. But with interplay between religions new possibilities emerge. The question of judging world-views becomes more existential: choice becomes just possible.

Moreover, most religions (that is, those which are old enough to proliferate) take diverse forms. Even if you think that you will be forever a Christian, and in that respect there is no question of choice, you may still have to decide what kind of a Christian you are going to be. Even within a given denomination there are varying styles and persuasions. And they each have different fruits.

Some people may claim that they do not have a faith — maybe not, if by that we mean some formal kind of religious identity or commitment. But does this mean that such people do not have some kind of worldview? They might turn out to be liberals, nationalists or anti-religious; or maybe Marxists, feminists or internationalists. They have worldviews or value-systems even if not religious ones. How are such so-called secular worldviews to be chosen and judged?

The meeting of religions and worldviews means that borrowings occur. For thirty years now or more — from the time of the startling sixties and before — you could find books on Zen Catholicism, Christian yoga, Buddhist–Jewish dialogue and the like. Hindus have absorbed notions from Western philosophy and Christian-missionary practice. Islamic modernism — that is, the attempt to indicate Islam's capacity to deal with the modern world — often borrows practical forms, such as non-traditional education, from the West. Most frequently religions get drawn into nationalism (itself basically a modern phenomenon of the last two or three hundred years), and so Orthodox Serbs may fight against Catholic Croats and Buddhist Sinhalese against Hindu Tamils. So we do not just have religions and value-systems, but various blends. This is sometimes condemned by conservatives as being syncretism. But never mind, it occurs. And we have to use judgement to determine whether we should take such criticism seriously.

Moreover, even the keenest fundamentalist, eager to proclaim the uniqueness and purity of his tradition, interprets the scripture in his own way. I have called such renditions of the faith "idiosyncretic", with a little pun: signifying that the preacher feeds his own unconscious into the texts, thus producing a new, but unrecognized blend. I always remember when Jimmy Carter was busy dismantling the Panama Canal treaties, that a preacher proclaimed that his action was contrary to the New Testament. What did Paul know about the Panama Canal? The interpretation of the preacher had to come from his own depths or from his social milieu or both.

The pattern of this book

This introductory chapter sets the scene. It is obvious,

however, that we cannot discuss questions of judging choices, without having a sketch at least of what the choices are. So Chapter 2 will paint in briefly the range of religions and worldviews which exist in our global world. It has to be an impressionist painting, this: we can certainly not put in the tiny details. The point is not to strive for completeness, but rather to give the reader a general orientation. Because of the blendings and rivalries between secular and religious worldviews, something has to be said too about the former in our portrait of global value-systems. Nor should we forget new religions arising all the time: maybe the configuration of our future world will be very different. Had an observer looked at the Roman Empire in 100 C.E., how could she have predicted the huge success to come of that new religion called Christianity? Or had she looked at Judaism in 60 C.E. how could she have intuited its future transformation once the Temple had been razed? Who could have realized how Buddhism would come to change the whole Far East, had she been observing it in 100 B.C.E. in Sri Lanka?

Actually this book is, in its own tiny way, part of the transformation of the global scene. Before the late twentieth century scarcely any one would have spoken of choosing a faith. This book is, in its own way, more or less unprecedented. If more and more people stand back from religions and look at them with objectivity and empathy, and then try to judge them, that already is a change. In 1993, there was opened in Glasgow, Scotland, a new museum of comparative religion, perhaps the first of its kind in the world. It contains a beautiful and sometimes uncanny plethora of works of art and ritual. I happened to have been advisor to the project. When it opened the Moderator of the Church of Scotland assaulted it somewhat. There was the implication that Christian objects and history should not be displayed alongside those of other faiths: it demeaned the True Faith. It was as if Christianity could not stand up for itself. But in our plural world it has to. The incident itself reveals a vital issue. Who is to tell what the True Faith is? About that issue I shall write a little later. But in the meantime the warm impartiality displayed towards so many different manifestations of religion poses questions to the large stream of visitors coming into such a museum.

So it is that I shall attempt to give an empathetic and objective view of the world's religions and worldviews in short compass. Because of globalization, this begins to delineate the choices we have (that is, that privileged "we", who exist beyond the realms of poverty and ignorance which afflict so much of the global population).

Now the reaction of many, faced with choice and an encounter with the world's faiths can be: perhaps they all point to the same truth. That makes choice an affair of taste and convenience. Well, maybe the faiths do point to the One. Some important people have thought so: Vivekananda, Aldous Huxley, John Hick and others. Whether or not such people are right, it is important to know the extent to which religions agree. That at least reduces the scope of choice. It is important also for other reasons. If faiths of diverse revelations and civilizations agree, this may tell us something about humanity. For instance, that similar religious experiences recur in different civilizations. It might tell us something too about the Ultimate. That it, or she, or he is revealed in more than one civilization. At any rate, the second chapter is followed by one that attempts to depict the degree to which religions and worldviews agree (or disagree).

Next, we get to matters of judgement proper. Religions are, in part, ideas — and in part teachers, who are some of the most important sources of ideas. I raise questions as to how we can evaluate them. And again, who are we? Can we just stand outside a tradition and give its ideas and sources good or bad marks? Perhaps sometimes our judgements need to be hypothetical: if you favour peace then such and such a religion is good; but maybe realistically we sometimes need to use force, in which case.... And so on.

In the following chapter I shall turn more directly to the practical side of religion, and above all its ethical aspect (but other practical dimensions such as ritual also need to be taken into account). *By their fruits ye shall know them.* Though again this is not a straightforward matter since fruits may vary. If one tree produces apples and another oranges we may count up how many each brings forth: but at the end of the day there is the issue of how we compare oranges and apples.

Finally, we look at religions and worldviews from a global

perspective. The fact is that humans have to live together. Times are too dangerous for us to allow conflicts to fester and abound. Weapons of mass destruction, above all nuclear bombs, are gradually spreading to country after country. Sooner or later there may be a vastly destructive clash. The continuation of the human race is by no means assured. Our value-systems should be adapted to living together harmoniously, even where profound divergences of belief may exist. I shall consider problems of lessening tensions in the final chapter. This may turn out to be one of the most vital tests of a worldview — the light it may shed on how we are to live together successfully. This, then, in outline is the pattern of this book. And now some reflections about judging.

The outsider becomes an insider

My favourite Native American proverb is "Never judge a person without walking a mile in his moccasins". It is evidently futile to judge something or somebody when you are totally out of sympathy with it or her. Or rather out of empathy. If sympathy means having the same feelings and so being "pro" someone; and antipathy means having contrary feelings and so being "con", then what we need for understanding is empathy — being able to enter another person's feelings and viewpoint. At the end of the day you may come to love or hate that person; but in the meantime you must be able to enter into her feelings. Often our education is poor at mustering our imaginative resources to practise empathy. But it is important. In order to understand

Hitler's appeal, we should be able to imagine what it was like to be a German after Germany's defeat after World War I and during the Depression. You might disapprove of the German's feelings but you should be able to imagine and enter into them. Likewise in order to understand the Kennedy era, you should be able to empathize with the hopes and excitement of many Americans. You might approve or you might not — but you should be able to understand.

In religious matters such empathy is not always easy to achieve. On the contrary: far too much of our schooling neglects "the other". It is important, however, if you are not a Jew but looking at Judaism, to come to appreciate the special feeling which the Orthodox Jew has for the Sabbath. You have its rituals — the gathered family, the sacred meal, the candles, the walk to the synagogue, the greeting of friends, the service, the singing, the leadership of the rabbi — and so on. It needs empathy: and it also needs quite a lot of information. And so, if the outsider is to become a kind of insider, it requires *informed* empathy.

It is a bit like the case of games (to go from the sublime to the engaging). If I do not understand the rules of basketball and feel no enthusiasm on seeing it on my television screen, and am prejudiced anyway, perhaps because the players are too tall for my taste (I being of medium size and so liable to feel disadvantaged) — then it is unwise for me to express any serious judgement about it.

Not only should we cultivate informed empathy in order to practise comparative religion, or more broadly the exploration of worldviews, but we should if possible achieve balance. If all you know about a religious view is its doctrines, and nothing about its rituals and ethics or about the experiences and emotions which animate it, or about its role in the social world, or about its art and the like, then you do not have a balanced view. Out of context, it may turn out that the doctrines become meaningless. If you are told that a Buddhist believes that everything is impermanent, but you know nothing of the meditation practices which give this philosophical claim life, then already you have not seen a balanced picture of the religion. In my sketches of the world's religions and worldviews I shall try to paint in something of the various dimensions of each faith or sub-faith, in order at least to hint at the needed balance.

And so to sum up: in approaching a religion we should strive for at least a modicum of balanced and informed empathy. A friend of mine, teaching in a university in which quite a number of the students are Islamic, was trying to introduce them to Christianity as part of a world religions course. He asked them to try and think what it would be like to be a Christian — say a Catholic attending Mass. At first the Muslim students were a bit resistant. He then suggested they should try to do this at least for twenty minutes. Then they learned that he was not trying to con them into being Christians, but just to use their imaginations.

You have, temporarily, to become a bit of an insider in order to judge another faith; but then you need to use your judgement. Nothing in this procedure of becoming a bit of an insider demands any change of religion or worldview on your part. But it may alter some of your perceptions. There is nothing disloyal in this, if, that is, you care about loyalty to your existing commitment.

The fruits of reflecting about values

If you become better informed about traditions or values other than your own it may well alter your attitudes and perceptions. You might, if you are not a traditionally practising Jew, think that the rules about food, so complex and so arbitrary to your mind, are rather ridiculous. But try to enter into their meaning. Feeding is a basic activity. If you then find that out of loyalty to your tradition you cannot eat meat and milk together, and must eschew pork and shellfish, and need special kitchen arrangements and so on, you will begin to appreciate that these rules obtrude on much of your time. And already you begin to see their point. They are not rules made up by a club or a sorority. They emanate (in orthodox Jewish faith) from the Lord. They are a constant reminder of God. Their observance signifies loyalty to a covenant, or agreement, entered into by your people with the Lord. The rules therefore are a practical and constant reminder of the existence of, and relationship with, the one God. Understanding all this may help you to judge Judaism better. Moreover, the truth about Judaism is not just the externals: it is the attitude and feelings of practising Jews. If you don't get inside the phenomenon you are distorting it. And so in following the path of informed empathy you are approaching the heart of the very phenomenon that you may wish to judge. All this implies a certain change of attitude.

It is said that to understand all is to forgive all. Maybe so, though I can imagine cases where understanding might lead to greater outrage. What if you think that your son was killed by someone because he had slept with that person's wife, and you then find that the person who killed him did so just for a bet? Nevertheless, understanding may soften attitudes: there is a greater inclination among those who have studied religion or known people of another faith to be more tolerant. The same may be true of reflecting about religions from a philosophical perspective. It should lead at least to a certain softening of claims. Let me explain.

You meet a person of very strong faith. She is not only certain in her commitments, but she also holds that her knowledge of the world as received from the Bible is certain. I make the distinction, because you can hold to a position which you know does not command universal acceptance (for instance, you know people who are otherwise pretty rational but hold opposing beliefs; and you may recognize that you cannot *prove* your worldview); and yet "know" in your bones that your worldview is best, and you act upon it. We can call these two aspects of a faith position: certainty is what you do not profess to have about your worldview, and certitude is what you do have. The one is a certain kind of theoretical certainty, the other, practical certainty.

Now it seems to me that a preliminary reflection about religious and secular worldviews leads to the conclusion that there is no public, provable certainty in them. In Jainism (an ancient and important religion of India) there is a philosophical position known as *syadvada*. Literally this could be rendered as "Maybe-ism". You should always utter a cautionary "It may be" before your utterances. It is a wise thought: scientists were once certain that continental shift theory was a lot of garbage — they learned later that their denial of the theory was the real garbage; most of what was once taught as science is now seen to be outdated; the Soviet Union which was predicted to last many decades suddenly collapsed; older histories keep getting rewritten and so on. So, to return to my initial thesis, I would ask how you would prove something in a religion or worldview.

There is no God? Maybe there is no God, but how do you prove it? Climb outside the universe and take a look? There is a wonderful story about Gagarin after his first trip in space. Khruschev drew him aside at a Kremlin reception in his honour. "Tell me, Major Gagarin," he enquired, "was it just empty space up there, or was He there?" Gagarin replied: "I'm sorry to tell you, Comrade Khruschev, but He was." Khruschev then told him, "I thought He might be, but this must remain an Inner Party Secret, you understand." Later, on a world tour, Gagarin was invited to the Vatican for a reception. The Pope drew him to one side and asked him, "When you were up there was God there, or not?" Gagarin was about to answer that He was, when he remembered that it was an Inner Party Secret. "I'm sorry to have to tell you this," he said, "but He wasn't." The Pope answered "Well, shall we keep it to ourselves?"

Of course the whole tale is ridiculous, since God inhabits a different sphere of existence and is not to be found floating about beyond the clouds. Could even Gagarin have got to that transcendent region? So, if you can't climb out of the cosmos, you won't show conclusively that God doesn't exist.

Or can you show that Christ is divine? Let us say that the Bible says so, and the Bible is certainly true. But a conclusion is as good or bad as the strength of its premise. How can you be certain that the Bible is true? Is it your faith? But the Muslim has equal faith in the Qur'an, and while the two books often agree, sometimes they disagree. They cannot both be certainly true. Or is it that the Bible agrees with known historical facts? First, many historians would be doubtful about this, to put it mildly. Second, many of the arguments are, of their nature — whether we were talking about the Bible or any other document — merely inferential. You can therefore have certitude about the Bible but not public certainty. But you can have certitude, on the basis of the Bible, about Christ.

But you might believe in Christ because of a powerful experience of him, or of being healed in his name. But do not such certitudes arise concerning celestial Buddhas?

I am not in any way saying here that faith in Christ is false: but its exclusivity and certainty cannot be established. That is, except on the basis of faith — but here we are not in the public realm of proof. It is not strange that faith is unprovable. That, after all, is its nature. Nor does this fact detract from the power of religion and the riches it can display. Religions are what they are independently of what can be proved. They are their own proof.

Reflection on all this might lead to more toleration. We can respect the faith of others. Further, it may lead us in the direction of thinking more about power than orthodoxy. What is important about a worldview is its power to affect lives and the fabric of society. The power to bring vision to existence, to nurture good behaviour and deep attitudes to others, to animate compassion, to generate holiness, to give hope. One of the fruits of reflection is seeing that by their fruits a faith can be judged.

All this applies to secular ideologies as well as to sacred worldviews. Nationalism, for example: no doubt it has worth in organizing a people's spirit. It provides life and vigour to a national entity. But it can also breed hatreds. Most wars are fought for nationalist reasons, which also lie behind many of the cruelties peoples inflict on one another. Beating Germany at football is one thing: dying amid the poppies of Flanders is another. Or take liberal economics: its release of energies through free trade and the empowerment of entrepreneurs is fine. But its failures with the homeless and the mentally unprepared, its unemployment lines, its disregard for failures — these fruits are more bitter.

Marxism has provided the most ludicrous and maybe the most tragic episode of modern history. Its brave new world destroyed peasants, created vast pollutions, made the proletariat into new serfs, crippled the creative middle-class spirit, shackled poets and novelists, painters and musicians (musicians less, because music is not easily read by censors), generated gulags, poured far too much concrete. Its pathetic achievements were offset by its ability to muster men and women for war. Yet it did have vision, before it was tried. It did sometimes nurture considerable faith and dedication.

Reflection about human worldviews, whether religious or secular, has various outcomes, to one or two of which we have alluded already. By exploring, however briefly, different worldviews we have a better understanding of global politics and culture. It probably brings a greater sense of toleration. It becomes more difficult, for instance, to exclude the plural exploration of religion in schools. Also, the need for empathy is important in its own right beyond the understanding of religions: it represents a mode of the imagination which is relevant to all of the humanities and social sciences. Reflection may also introduce other values, for it raises questions about consistency.

For the fact of the matter is that successful traditions are defined as those which live through quite a number of epochs. A tradition needs to adapt to changes of knowledge. It is one of the virtues of a tradition that it has the resilience to do this: and estimating its success, for instance in harmonizing with science (itself intensely revisionary), is one of the tasks of reflection. Here of course, we are involved in issues about consistency, and so information, empathy and logic all become ingredients of reflection.

Filling out the idea of balance

We have noted that balance is important in understanding a faith. My own formula for dealing with this is through a list of what I call the dimensions of religion. In my brief account of religions and, more generally, worldviews, I shall use this list to indicate a balanced view of each.

By dimensions I mean: doctrines, narratives, ethics, experiences, rituals, organizations and materials. Or I could put all this a bit more broadly by saying: doctrines and philosophy; narratives and histories; ethics and law; experiences and emotions; rituals and practices; organizations and social effects; materials and artistic objects. For instance, in Christianity there are various beliefs, most notably the Trinity doctrine, that God is three persons in one substance (Father, Son and Holy Spirit). Christianity has the narratives of the Old and New Testaments and of the history of the Church. It has ethical injunctions, such as the Ten Commandments and Christ's teaching of love. It nurtures the experience of God's response to prayer and feelings of exaltation and peace. It has the rituals of the Eucharist and of preaching, amongst others. It has produced the complex organization of the Church (or rather many sects of such organizations, from the Catholics to the Quakers). It has generated huge cathedrals, plain chapels, ikons, sculptures and so forth.

Or take the example of Buddhism in Sri Lanka (Theravada Buddhism). This has the doctrine or philosophy that everything is impermanent, but that liberation from this suffering world can be achieved, viz. nirvana. It has the story of the Buddha, his previous lives, the history of the faith. It has the ethic of harmlessness and compassion. It has the experience of meditation for adepts, and serenity for lay persons. It has the rituals of venerating the Buddha and going on pilgrimage. It has the Sangha, or Order of monks, and a long tradition of national solidarity. It has temples, sacred trees, Buddha-statues and so on.

It is possible to tie the dimensions together. The divinity of Christ makes sense of the ritual of the Eucharist. The ethic of love ties in with the perfect unity of the Trinity. The narrative of creation, the Fall and Israel leads up to the doctrine of salvation through Christ's self-sacrifice (and in that connection ritual is of course central). And so on.

There could be other ways of achieving balance, for example, by listing an alternative set of dimensions. But the achievement of a list is to discourage any thin or one-dimensional account of Christianity. It is not just a set of beliefs: much, much more indeed.

Another aspect of balance is that we do not identify a multiple religion with any one branch of that religion. If you ask a Baptist what the Christian faith is, she may give you an account which is simply Baptist. This will not be balanced from a historical and descriptive perspective. I am not here commenting on truth; trying to ascertain the True Faith involves various value-judgements and expressions of particular faith. But I am urging that there are other reputable (or even less than reputable) forms of the Christian tradition which also demand to be heard.

Roman Catholicism, for instance, has an entirely different tradition from that of Baptists. If someone genuinely wishes to know what Christianity is, and views this as a descriptive and historical question, then we need to give a realistic answer in terms of the phenomena characterized as Christianity: the Catholics, the Orthodox, the Protestants — first the magisterial reformation (Lutherans, Calvinists, Anglicans), and second the radical reformers (Mennonites or Anabaptists, Quakers, Congregationalists, Unitarians and so on). Then there are faiths which lie at the edge of the tradition as often understood: Mormonism, Christian Science, Unificationism and so on. Adherents of these faiths typically wish to be called Christian, and it is not for us, from a historical or descriptive angle, to deny them the title.

Let me finish off my general point of view about balance in

this second sense. What we need to convey is the richness and complexity of the tradition (of any tradition). Choices are not made just between traditions but also within them.

Actually things are a good deal more complex than I have indicated. For there can be ideological divisions within the broader Church, which can cut across denominational or sectarian boundaries. For instance, scriptural conservatives can be found in quite a number of denominations as well as "modernists" or liberals. This is an extra divide from that found between denominations. Moreover, persons of the same denomination can differ through their nationalism. Sri Lankan, Burmese, Cambodian, Laotian and Vietnamese Buddhists impart their respective flavours to the whole mass of Theravadic custom and faith.

And so we need to bear in mind that traditions and subtraditions have their variations.

There is one other major comment that I would like to make. It is important to bear in mind that all the major religions have undergone great changes in the last two or three hundred years, because of the onset of industrialism in some countries and colonialism in the rest of the world. The expansion of Europe in America led to the consolidation of overseas empires: in Latin America first, in North America, in India, in South-East Asia, in East Asia, in the Pacific and in Africa. This meant that indigenous religions and cultures had to adapt, in order to retain tradition while making such changes as could help them meet the Western challenge.

For instance, the Hindu tradition consolidated itself in new ideological ways through famous English-speaking writers such as Vivekananda, Gandhi and Radhakrishnan. In various ways this neo-Hindu philosophy, combining with practical modernizing, created the shape of modern India. Some cultures borrowed overheavily from the West: China for instance used an adapted Marxism to establish a strong national independence, but wiped out much of its tradition. At any rate, the point is that we are not, in the modern world, looking at religions as they were in ancient or medieval times, but rather as transformed traditions which have passed through the fires of colonialism and modernization. Often they react against some of these forces (for instance some forms of fundamentalism are experimenting with a new way of trying to be conservative).

There are, then, three kinds of balance in dealing with religions: one is to do with dimensionality; another with varieties; and a third with religions as they are today, to balance our picture of them as ancient. It is a little like the way we treat another human being. You may know her well at work, but know nothing of her husband or children or outside interests. That is like the question of dimensionality. You might know another person only when on her best behaviour, but you may know nothing about her tantrums or depressions. This is like the question of variety. You may know her now, but know nothing of her past. Or it may be that you knew a man at college, but scarcely recognize him now, with all the changes in character that have taken place.

In the same way religions must be seen against the back- ground of the great transformations that have happened in and through the world in the last two hundred years or so.

This, finally, may remind us about the future. It is always hazardous to predict what is to come. But it would not be surprising if religions were to change greatly as the global scene becomes consolidated. They will change through having to treat of one another. They will change because human life will alter, no doubt radically. They will change in response to new forms of knowledge and perhaps to the discovery of new kinds of spirituality. If we are optimistic we may think that the best of the faiths is yet to come. Why not? Why do we always look back in matters of religion, and not forward to promises as yet unrealized? At any rate, I now turn to my brief description of the religions and secular worldviews of our global civilization.

CHAPTER TWO
A MAP OF THE WORLD'S RELIGIONS

Three regions have been particularly vital in the generation of major religions. One is the Middle East and Europe, which has given birth to Judaism, Christianity and Islam, not to mention Greek and Roman philosophy and Zoroastrianism. Another is South Asia, parent of Buddhism, Jainism, Hinduism and Sikhism. The third is East Asia with its offspring Taoism and Confucianism, as well as Shinto. It also had its transforming effects on Mahayana Buddhism.

Other regions are important, but in different ways. South-East Asia saw a flowering of Theravada Buddhism, in an abiding contact with Sri Lanka. Africa created a plethora of religious manifestations in sub-Saharan (Black) Africa, though this has been greatly overlaid by the establishment of Christianity and Islam as the chief outside faiths, rapidly becoming indigenized in various ways (e.g. in the creation of new African independent churches and the like). In the Americas indigenous religions were somewhat, though not wholly, crushed by the weight of Catholicism south of the Rio Grande, and of Protestantism to the north. Likewise the Pacific region had a very strong impact on Christianity, throughout the islands and in Australia and New Zealand. Similar remarks apply to Europe and North Asia, from Lapland to Vladivostok, where many shamanistic and small-scale religions have weakened or disappeared.

I began with a region which has generated faiths. We should not identify their earlier habitat with their present-day profusion. For instance, Islam has not only spread throughout the Arab world and along the southern layer of the old Roman Empire, but into Central Asia, South Asia, and above all in South-East Asia, where Malaysia and Indonesia are predominantly Islamic nations — the latter being by far the largest Muslim nation. The vast majority of Muslims are in South and South-East Asia — about 600 million; with substantial numbers in Central Asia and China. Likewise the demographic balance of Christianity is slipping southwards. Africa and Latin America, together with North America, are its most important regions (though a revived Russian and Eastern European Orthodoxy should not be neglected). Christianity has strong footholds in Asia — in the Philippines, Korea and Vietnam particularly. Judaism through much of its history has flourished outside its ancient home — in Europe and the Islamic world, for instance. But the tragedy of the Holocaust and the migration of Jews from the Islamic world have radically changed the picture. Now the two greatest centres of Judaism are Israel and the United States (though there are not unimportant populations in Russia, and elsewhere).

Another important fact about the modern world, especially after World War II, is the great mixing of peoples. You can find significant numbers of:

Yorubas from West Africa in Los Angeles;
Sikhs in Birmingham, England;
Parsees (Zoroastrians) in Bombay;
Greek Orthodox in Sydney, Australia;
Chinese Buddhists in Toronto;
Hindus in South Africa;
Confucianists in Berkeley, California;
Turkish Muslims in Frankfurt;
Mormons in Fiji;
Tibetan Buddhists in Scotland;
Muslims in Bradford, England...
and so on.

Thus religions are increasingly growing diasporas, that is populations outside their more traditional habitat. All this increases the daily pluralism of life in traditional societies. During the colonial epoch Indians could not ignore missionary Christianity: now Christians "at home" cannot ignore Islam and Buddhism.

Another phenomenon in today's world (more so than at other times because of the rapidity of global changes and because of the aftermath of colonialism) is the multiplying of new religious movements. I have already mentioned the numerous new independent churches in Africa. But there are quite a number of new Japanese religions, as well as new movements in America, ranging from Mormons and Unificationists to Hare Krishna followers and what is loosely known as New Age; new prophetic movements among Native Americans; Siberian religions; and others. All this adds to the great cornucopia of religions great and small which the Earth has brought forth.

There are also secular worldviews to consider. Of all modern value-systems the most important must be nationalism. The idea of the nation-state has spread from America and Europe to the rest of the world. It is imperfectly expressed because the theory is that every nation should have its state: should have "'freedom". Naturally, since nations can be ruled by iron parties and great dictators, equipped most frequently with censors and torturing police, freedom for the individual in no way coincides with that of the nation. But nationalism has forged new identities and given both a sense of belonging and a unity through which to administer industry, welfare and so on. Big nations forge empires (in other words rule) on a wide scale over other ethnic groups, who under the oppression of imperialism demand their own national independence. This is why nationalism spread so easily from Europe to other, overseas countries, and within Europe throughout the Habsburg and Ottoman Empires.

Often you had to shape your nation, by creating or

perfecting a national language, through exploring and setting forth the country's history, through writing national music: think of Chopin, Dvorak, Liszt, Verdi, Grieg, Sibelius, Tchaikovsky, Wagner.... To assist you in your making of a nation came universal education: the young could learn the national narrative (or myth), the language, loyalty to the flag, and so forth. Nationalism became a kind of religion alongside religion. Sometimes the two blended most formidably. To be Romanian and Orthodox were nearly the same. To be Protestant and American for long had a symbiosis. In latter days, to be Marxist and Albanian were to be the same. Often religions came to be dynamic boosters of the national spirit, as well as secular ideologies. Maoism came to be the spur of Chinese nationalism (indeed imperialism).

Nationalism contains a multitude of worldviews, since each nation has different national values and histories typically supported by somewhat different ideologies. It has its own, though parallel, rituals.

It is easy for us in the last decade of the twentieth century, having witnessed the collapse of Marxism in the West, and seeing it eroded somewhat in China, Vietnam and elsewhere, to underestimate the power it exerted for most of the period after World War II. For fifty years it was apparently immovable. And for seventy years or more it dominated the huge Soviet Empire. It helped to shape institutions and lives. As an Empire, the Marxist system kept a cork on the fizzing bottle of nationalities. Perhaps its days are really gone: but we shall consider it briefly later on. It has lessons for us all.

If Marxism was an errant child of the so-called European Enlightenment, another was the liberal ethos of democratic individualism. The latter does not fit very naturally into the ethos of the nation. It often has done so through the bridge of capitalism. It produces a mobile workforce, much social fluidity, and a consumer society — all of which favor individualism — while nations are often intended to be large enough to provide the substructure and milieu for large-scale enterprise. (For instance, there was debate in the first half the nineteenth century as to whether Belgium was big enough to be a separate country: as it turned out it proved to be highly successful at industrialization.) But of course individualism had much deeper roots in Kant and in utilitarianism, in the quest for human rights, and in struggles against collectivism.

Now liberal individualism can easily combine with certain religions, particularly with Protestantism. It becomes a separate worldview when it combines with agnosticism or atheism to form what is often known as scientific humanism. The latter places the highest priority in value on human beings, while it sees knowledge of this world flowing solely from the pursuit of science. In more recent times there has been much greater concern in the West (following Jain Buddhist and other examples) for the rights of animals. This concern for all life forms might be called *bionism*.

Broadly speaking, the major worldviews other than traditionally religious ones are: the varieties of nationalisms, Marxism, individualism and scientific humanism. They are sometimes in alliance with traditional religions, but mostly not.

Modes of Belief and practice

The big trio from the Middle East are more or less pure monotheisms. Judaism was of course the leader in this: it welded together a faith focused on a single Lord and creator of the cosmos, who entered into a covenant or agreement with his special people. This involved two forms of Torah or teaching: the written, which makes up the first five books of the Hebrew Scriptures, and the oral Torah which was handed down in the community from Sinai. After the destruction of the Temple in 70 C.E. by the Romans, Judaism began to take shape under the leadership of rabbis, adhering to the Law, performing synagogue worship, maintaining the identity of the people and preserving their scriptures, including the first five books, the writings of prophets and other material, together with the hugely expanding Talmud, a detailed guide to traditional oral Torah. Sometimes persecuted under both Christian and Islamic rule and often treated as second class citizens from Spain to Russia, in due course the Jews emerged from the ghetto to participate in the eighteenth century Enlightenment and the nineteenth century migration to America and elsewhere. This generated a crisis and a division of Judaism into three

broad movements: the Orthodox which is somewhat fundamentalist; the Reform, a kind of liberal Judaism stressing
ethical monotheism; and Conservative Judaism, more liberal in opinion than the Orthodox, but committed to following
the Law in detail. Woven into Jewish life from the end of
the nineteenth century was Zionism, culminating in the
foundation of the State of Israel. Great impetus to migration to Israel was given by the horrors of the Holocaust during the Nazi period.

As far as dimensions go, in broad brush strokes we can
depict Judaism as involving: doctrine — belief in one Lord
and Creator; narrative — the story of the Jewish people i.e.
its covenant with God, its destiny as a Light to the Gentiles,
its survival despite persecutions and terrible suffering;
ethics and law — its adherence to God's commandments;
experience — the vivid awareness of God among the
prophets and the mysticism in the Kabbalah tradition and
among the still influential Hasidim; ritual — its faithfulness
to the Sabbath, holy days, synagogue and family worship;
organization — its congregational solidarity under the rab-
binic leadership; material manifestation — its synagogue
buildings.

Christianity, though an offshoot of Judaism, and therefore
believing in one God and the Old Testament, took a very
different form. Because it believed in the divinity of Christ
and of the Holy Spirit, it came to evolve the Trinity doctrine:
that God is Three in One. It took up elements of Greek
philosophy. It had its own more centralized organization,

and a pattern of monasticism, cultivating meditation, learning and farming. In its Western half it grew a central Papacy in Rome. Eastern Orthodoxy drifted away from Western Catholicism, believing itself to be the true and original faith. In the West in the sixteenth century, the Reformation unfolded a new dynamism, eventually doing away with many of the externals of Catholicism in an attempt to return to pure and Biblical Christianity.

Dimensionally, all three branches, with a very few exceptions in the Protestant branch, believe in the Trinity and the saving work of Christ; in narrative, all hold to the story of God's guidance of Israel and foundation of a new Israel, the Church. Later history is variously interpreted. In ethics, the supreme value is Love, which mirrors the Trinity. Experientially, both Orthodoxy and Catholicism value the inexpressible inner life, kept alive above all in the monasteries and convents; and Protestants especially value conversion as a prelude to a new life. Ritually, the Mass, liturgy and Communion are central over much of Christianity, but the more radical Protestants favour the centrality of the preaching of God's Word.

Organizationally, Catholicism is a monarchy, with cardinals, bishops and priests in a single hierarchy; Orthodoxy has leading bishops or patriarchs in different countries, bishops and priests; Anglicanism and Lutheranism have a similar organization, but other Protestants tend to be more democratic and congregational in their self-management. The artefacts of Christianity range from vast cathedrals to simple

Protestant chapels; while ikons seen as "windows on heaven" form a vital focus of much Orthodox piety.

Islam draws on both the Jewish and Christian past. Jesus is seen as the last of the prophets before Muhammad, the Seal or culmination of the Prophets. Muhammad received God's revelation, the Qur'an, an Arabic copy of an everlasting work in heaven, God's thoughts and message for humankind. The faith is dated from 622 C.E., when Muhammad began his transition from his native Mecca to Medina, where he set up the first Islamic commonwealth. Eventually the faith spread rapidly not only across Arabia but into the whole of the Middle East and North Africa, and in due course into Central Asia, South Asia, Malaysia and Indonesia, West Africa and elsewhere. It is divided into two broad denominations, plus some less important movements. The more orthodox call themselves traditionalists, namely the Sunni (Sunna) and the Shi'i (Denominationalists). The latter are particularly important in Iran and Iraq, as well as parts of the eastern Mediterranean, but are, overall, in a minority in Islam. Other groups are the Alawi, Druze and Isma'ili movements. A "heretical" form of Islam is the Ahmadiya, in Pakistan and elsewhere.

Dimensionally, in doctrine Islam believes in One God and Muhammad as his messenger; in narrative, Islam harks back to Abraham and others. But the major concern is with the life of Muhammad, expressed in a large number of stories, the Hadith. Ethically, Islam mingles morality and the law provision or Shari'a of a new society. They see the spectacular political and military successes of especially earlier Islam as a sign of God's guidance. Experientially important is a sense of the abiding and continuous presence of God. Also vital in Islam was the tradition of Sufis, or mystics, who formed brotherhoods to cultivate the life of prayer and meditation. Ritually, daily prayer is mandatory at determined intervals; people should also, if they can, go on pilgrimage to Mecca at least once. Organizationally there is no real hierarchy, but experts on law and religion form an elite; while in Shi'a Islam, learned people come to be regarded as Ayatollahs who gain great prestige. They interpret the leadership of the last of a series of Imams who has gone into occultation till he shall reappear in history. The Aga Khan has a kind of monarchical role within the Isma'iliya. Meanwhile in theory the whole of the Muslim community should be under the general rule of the Caliph — but the Caliphate, centred in Istanbul, was abolished after World War I.

In modern times dynamic new forces, typified by the Muslim Brotherhood in Egypt, have emerged stimulating a modernised, pious, conservative and yet radical Islam.

The fourth great religion in the first area is, or was, Zoroastrianism. Not only was it over long periods the faith of the Persian Empire: it has persisted, admittedly very much as a minority, both in Iran and abroad, especially in Western India as the faith of the Parsees. Its doctrines and myths have greatly contributed to all three of the great monotheisms. Its picture of a world in which the Creator

God is opposed by an evil rebellious force contributed to the idea of the Devil (Satan); its picture of a future judgement and the resurrection of the dead entered into the three faiths; it also provided its own form of ethical monotheism.

South Asia has its own monotheism. But its most successful religion, Buddhism, is not theistic. Buddhism has permeated virtually the whole of Asia east of Iran, even if it greatly faded in India itself (but not in South Asia — it flourishes in Sri Lanka, parts of Nepal, and in Tibet, even if persecuted under Chinese rule). It has no place for a Creator God or even for a determinate beginning of the cosmos. Its attention was initially fixed on the attainment of nirvana, or liberation from the round of rebirth. It represents a new non-orthodox movement, outside of the fold of Brahmin orthodoxy; and held to belief in rebirth or reincarnation which later came to permeate Hindu belief. Ethical living, self-awareness and meditation can lead to ultimate liberation.

Theravada Buddhism, or the Teaching of the Elders, found in Sri Lanka and South-East Asia, keeps to these teachings but elsewhere Buddhism developed further, in the Great Vehicle or Mahayana. Here the figure of the Bodhisattva or the Buddha-to-be grew in importance: a person should put off his liberation till all are freed. Compassion for others rules the Bodhisattva's heart. Some Bodhisattvas came to be seen as merciful saviours, as well as celestial Buddhas, such as Amitabha (in Japan, Amida), creator of a paradise for those who are faithful to him. Beyond Mahayana lie Tantric or ritualized forms of Buddhism, notably in Tibet and

Mongolia. This is sometimes treated as a third major division, the Vajtayana, or Diamond Vehicle.

Dimensionally, Buddhism has the philosophy of the impermanence of everything in the cosmos; narratively, it concentrates on the life and previous lives of the Buddha Gautama, who taught the doctrine and the way of life in the fifth century B.C.E., and on the myths of the celestial Buddhas and Bodhisattvas; ethically, it teaches above all compassion; experientially, virtually all of Buddhism presents methods for the purification of consciousness leading to release; ritually, the veneration of the Buddha and the worship of Buddhas and Bodhisattvas has come to be important, and in the Vajrayana the use of spiritual designs or mandalas and other techniques of ritual self-transformation; organizationally, Buddhism centres on the Sangha, or Order of monks and nuns, together with pious laypersons; finally its artefacts are seen in the elaborate Buddhist arts of the Theravada, the Far East, etc.; above all the serene Buddha statues which are perpetual reminders of the ideal of self-control and insight.

Jainism has similarities with Buddhism and was launched, or as Jains feel, relaunched, by the Buddha's contemporary Mahavira. It is much more austere: the monk or nun lives a life of severe asceticism. An ideal way is to give up eating. It is most rigorous in its practice of *ahimsa,* or non-injury towards all living beings. It remains a small minority in India (maybe 5 million people out of some 800 million), but it has been vital during some periods of Indian history.

Doctrinally, it is atheist. The cosmos, depicted as being in the shape of a huge human, with us at the waist, is surrounded by infinite space. Historically, it looks to Mahavira and a succession of predecessors, who refound the faith from time to time. Ethically, it is above all the religion of austerity and *ahimsa*. Experientially, while Jains practise meditation, this has less impact than in Buddhism. Ritually, temples provide occasions for reverencing the leaders, or Tirthankaras, such as Mahavira. But this is more as a spur to faithful living. A liberated soul cannot intervene any more in the world, but has risen to a perfectly pain-free state, immobile at the summit of the universe. Organizationally, Jainism like Buddhism has its Order, divided into two branches, whose differences, however, are minimal. Its artefacts are above all the wonderful statues of saints, completely naked, and so indifferent to worldly concerns, sometimes of colossal proportions.

Hinduism came to evolve into a complex federation of beliefs and practices. It included many of the features of Buddhism and Jainism: meditation (yoga), austerity, reincarnation, liberation, a sense of a vast and cyclically repetitious cosmos; but it also developed an elaborate caste system, a plethora of temples and worship of numerous gods, but above all the great ones — Vishnu, Shiva, Kali. By the same token it developed *bhakti* or loving adoration of God, a theology of grace, pilgrimages — especially to Benares, Hinduism's most holy city — and so on. In the colonial period it became more unified, at least in theory, especially through the neo-Hindu philosophy of Vivekananda and

Radhakrishnan, harking back to the eighth century non-dualistic Vendanta, which took up themes both from the Upanishads and the *Bhagavadgita* (The Song of the Lord). This philosophy saw all religions as pointing to the same One, and transcending their own particular forms of worship, at a higher level. This philosophy was important in shaping Indian nationalism, since Muslims, Christians, Parsees and others could join in it as well as Hindus. On the whole, Hinduism is a kind of monotheism, with a supreme Divine Being, conceived as refracted through the many gods, which are so many different manifestations of the One.

Dimensionally, it has a doctrine of unity in diversity, as well as of reincarnation and karma; narratively, it has the many myths and stories of the divine, including great epics — The *Ramayana* and the *Mahabharata*; ethically, it has universal norms as well as the more particular duties of each caste; experientially, it has strong traditions of meditation and yoga, as well as powerful feelings of *bhakti* or devotionalism; organizationally, the Brahmins as top class remain religiously dominant but over an immensely complex social and religious system; materially, Hinduism's most obvious manifestation is the huge number of temples great and small and its numerous places of pilgrimage.

Sikhism originated from attempts to merge the spirituality both of the Hindu and Muslim traditions, focusing on the one True God. It incorporated reincarnation, however, and eventually found it necessary to stand up to the Mughal

(Islamic) emperors of North India. Under a succession of Gurus, or leaders, they eventually formed themselves into a separate community with various external signs, such as unshorn hair (and so the turban to hold it together), beards, a dagger, etc. They used the writings of the Gurus and of the final "Guru", i.e. the scriptures, or "Granth Sahib". Sikhism centres as a faith on the Golden Temple in Amritsar, in the Punjab, India, the main homeland of the Sikhs.

When we move east to China we enter a very different civilization even if Buddhism's entry from the first Century C.E. brought greater affinities between it and India. Without doubt the most important figure in Chinese culture is that of K'ung, or Confucius, (a Latinized form invented by early Jesuit missionaries). The word "Confucianism" is used in two or three ways. At one level it means the philosophy of Confucius himself, together with that of other thinkers in the tradition. Sometimes people dispute that it can be called a religious worldview: Confucius' main interests were in education, politics and ethics, though he mentions Heaven, a pale form of God. At another level, Confucianism is a State cult, involving temples to Confucius and other sages, and culminating in the rituals prescribed for the Emperor. Sometimes it is taken to include also the various elements of folk religion, and family life, including the remembrance of ancestors.

A more complex form of the Confucian philosophy is Neo-confucianism, whose chief exponent was Chu Hsi (1130-1200 C.E.). This had a much more metaphysical flavour. It affirmed a Great Ultimate or spiritual Absolute, the inter-play of matter and form, the rhythmic processes of the female (yin) and male (yang) principles, and so on. It had an appeal to rival Buddhist and Taoist thinkers. It also gave a new role to methods of contemplation in the Confucian tradition.

By the second millennium Chinese religions were begin-ning to fuse or live together in fruitful symbioses. Hence the notion of the "Three Religions of China" — Confucianism, Taoism and Buddhism. Different elements were relevant to different aspects of life. Taoism started with the teachings of the legendary Lao-tsu, supposedly a contemporary of the Buddha, who composed the Tao-te Ching (The Classic of the Tao and its Virtue). This extraordinary document (one could perhaps say anthology) taught that one should harmo-nize with nature or the Tao (Way), and so act through not acting. Later a religion incorporating the anthology and rev-erence for Lao as an Immortal or god was generated, which evolved a pantheon constituting a kind of heavenly counter-part to the empire on earth. It was involved in the quest for long life, healing, alchemy, and in various folk rituals. It was often an anarchic force in Chinese society; and there are even Taoist elements in the thought of Mao Zedong.

The themes of harmony with nature and of acting through not acting entered into and blended with Buddhist ideas in the movement known as Meditation Buddhism, of Chinese provenance, viz. Ch'an (Japanese Zen, Korean Son).

Both Buddhism and Taoism had space for folk religion. So the three major teachings of China came to supply the various needs of the people and of government: Confucianism for administration and a public ethos; Taoism for worldly and medical concerns; Buddhism for spiritual satisfaction. Naturally all the religions overlapped in function. Confucian ancestor-reverence was not irrelevant to family prosperity, etc.

I shall deal with the three in one in describing the dimensions. Doctrinally, China has tended to see the ultimate in somewhat impersonal terms, as Heaven or the Great Ultimate or as the Dharma (Buddhist teaching concretized as a first principle) or as the Tao. Reincarnation doctrine has blended uneasily with indigenous belief in the survival of ancestors. Narratively, China has had a good sense of its continuous history, placing much value on sheer antiquity. In ethics, Confucianism has stressed *jen,* or humanness, with ideas of reciprocity and *li,* or correct behaviour, as staples of social living. Experientially, there is in later Neoconfucianism an emphasis on meditative knowledge; but this and a sense also of devotion have animated the various Buddhist schools. Ritually, ancestor and State cults are important; but so are the various Taoist rites both at a popular level and in the inward attempt to harness ritual to physical transformations. Organizationally, Taoism has its own church structure, Buddhism the Sangha, and Confucianism sees bureaucracy as a kind of manifestation of its values. Materially, Chinese art is in diverse ways an expression of values embodied in the three religions: for instance Taoist art shows a lot of emptiness: a lot of acting by not acting.

Much of this threefold culture was handed on to Korea and Japan. Confucianism and Buddhism were dominant in Korea. In Japan, Buddhism became the most vital and pervasive force. New forms arose there, such as Shinran's strong pietism and reliance on Amida's grace,and Nichiren's more nationalistic Buddhism inspired by loyalty to the famous scripture, the Lotus Sutra. The way of the gods was long an adjunct to Buddhism, but in the later nineteenth century became separated out as a Japanese ritual tradition which the Government established as demanding loyalty from Japanese citizens and as a mode of giving special national sacrality to the Imperial family. Its shrines inspire a sense of harmony with nature. Its myths give a unique central place to Japan in the creation of the universe.

While Buddhism has the chief role in Japanese religion and philosophy, it has its own flavour. Its Zen is more military and crisp than its Chinese counterpart. Its artistic ethos is barer. Pure Land Buddhism gives even greater emphasis in Japan than it does in China to grace, and to Amida complete initiative in saving those who but call on his name in faith. Nichiren Buddhism is more overtly nationalistic than any kind of Chinese Buddhism.

Meanwhile, certain cultural areas, such as Black Africa, Native America and Aboriginal Australia are emerging into a new self-consciousness. Although until modern times Africa scarcely had a unified mutual consciousness, since communications were difficult and distances great, there has, in this twentieth century, emerged a sense of Africanness, which goes beyond Africa itself to the lands beyond the Atlantic, in North and South America and the Caribbean, wherever people of African stock flourish. There are new religious movements, such as Santeria and Vodun (Voodoo), blending African and Christian elements, and in Africa itself not merely new forms of Christianity, merging traditional African motifs and those of the Bible, but also a revived interest in classical African religions. Similar blends and revivals can be seen elsewhere, in Papua New Guinea, among the Australian Aboriginals and among Native Americans in North America. Across the world there are new senses of tradition, born of a proud self-awareness of older cultures which have been somewhat crushed by the weight of colonialism and mission.

This, then, is a brief sketch of the many forms of worldview present in our world: and not only present in themselves but also in relation to one another. We are becoming conscious of the varieties of human commitments and cultural forms.

CHAPTER THREE

HOW RELIGIONS MAY AGREE

It is commonly said that each religion is unique. Christians for instance, make much of the uniqueness of Christ. Now while it is foolish to ignore all this, it is unwise also to make too much of it. I am a unique individual, a unique human being; but that does not mean that there cannot be comparisons between my and my brother's noses, nor that a doctor cannot compare my heartbeat to that of my neighbour. We all bear both similarities to and unlikenesses from one another. And as we have noted, resemblances may be vital in helping us in judging diverse faiths. If Mahayana meditation resembles Christian meditation, then if I hold to Christian values that may help me to be more positive towards Mahayana.

Let me begin with mysticism, or contemplation (as I prefer to call it). It is a not uncommon claim that diverse cases of mysticism in world religions exhibit a core similarity. Some have held this in a radical way (Stace; Smart) and others in a more moderate way (Zaehner; Underhill). Others deny real resemblances, holding that the difference of context makes for real differences of experience. But this thesis has problems. We can surely compare the sexual experience of a married woman in Uganda with that of a significant other in Los Angeles; or the experience of a Russian matron and a Sri Lankan Buddhist — even if we recognize that the cultural meanings of sex and marriage are rather diverse in the different nations mentioned. Do we suppose that what is felt sexually is utterly different? And so even if the cultural meaning of contemplation differs widely, as between the Chinese Buddhist and the Muslim Sufi, that by no means settles the argument. There may be a better case for saying that theistic mysticism is diverse from that of non-theistic contemplation. We might look at St John of the Cross and a Buddhist Theravadic contemplative as being at opposite poles. Let us entertain this thought for a moment. It still leaves open the possibility that Sufis, Christian contemplatives, Jewish Kabbalists and Hindu theistic yogis have like experiences. Most writers seem to think that they do, (as with Otto; Underhill; Eliot; and others). So we might have two main kinds of mysticism, one theistic and the other not — the latter most evident in Buddhism.

However, it is worth noting that an impersonal aspect is important in a great deal of theistic mysticism, if not all. It is notable that Christianity came to use Neoplatonist motifs in expressing the inexpressible. These emphasized the notion that mystical experience frequently lies simply beyond speech: God's uttermost nature is unutterable, indescribable, indefinable, incomprehensible. Such ideas in their different ways are put forth in the Christian, Sufi, Hindu and Jewish traditions. Now these claims — these ventures into the speechless — are what make some scholars and saints suppose that "atheistic,(e.g. Buddhist) speechlessness is no different from theistic ineffability — that what cannot be said cannot be said.

But if you approach light down a tunnel here rather than a tunnel there, does it make a difference? The logical conclusion, I would think, is that of course one route makes the feel of the place of arrival feel different from that of the other route. But yet the light can be the same. In other words both claims, that there is a difference and that there is no difference, are right. The 'righter' claim is no doubt the latter, but we should not neglect the former, for the following reason.

The theist is not of course only concerned with the mystical. If the only kind of religious experience were the contemplative, perhaps we would all be Theravada Buddhists. But the theistic idea is built upon the numinous: it stems from what Otto called the *mysterium tremendum et fascinans* — the mystery which is both frightening and fascinating (or if you prefer another translation "something which is both awe-inspiring and wonderfully attractive"). So for the theistic contemplative the great voice of the prophets speaks out of their perception of the whirlwind and the mystery. But for the Buddha no such perception accrued. He saw gods, but saw through them, or thought he saw through them. We need not here prejudge the issue. In the one case, the light at the end of the tunnel is seen through the colours of prophecy and devotion: in the other the light is seen through the darkness of purity, without the mystery. It would be wrong of us to come down dogmatically on one side or the other — but each side is plausible.

So either there is a core of mysticism across religions; or there are two flavours, one theistic and the other non-theistic. In either case we may suppose that there are deep resemblances between religions.

Rudolf Otto's famous book *The Idea of the Holy (Das Heilige)* came out towards the end of World War I, appropriately during the horrific thunder of the guns of Flanders and during the prelude to the sufferings of the Isonzo. He saw in the experience of the numinous the core of religion. Given what I have already written about the contemplative experience, and given that the numinous has a polar structure, being of the other, which is the *mysterium tremendum et fascinans*, it is reasonable to think of it as different in type from the mystical. It implies that there are two major kinds of religious experience (and maybe others). Otto was of course correct to think of the Holy as central to many religious modes of experiences and attitude; but wrong to think of it as the only form. In fact, his treatment of the contemplative mode was defective since he could not properly handle the notion of union. The contemplative mode in alliance with the Other contributes to the concept of union. How can there be a union except with an Other? In the Theravada and certain other mystical religions, without the sense of the Other the notion of union does not arise.

NB

But Otto rightly points to analogies between the numinous experience in different contexts — the theophany accorded to Arjuna in the *Gita*, that found in Job when God speaks out of a whirlwind, the conversion of Paul on the Damascus Road and so forth: his book is replete with examples. These experiences help to account for the sense of holy Otherness which is found typically in descriptions of God — in the Jewish, Muslim, Christian, Hindu and other traditions.

And so it is not altogether surprising that there are convergences between the various Gods (even when they are not related: of course the three Western monotheisms do share the same heritage). Apart from the Otherness of God there is the growing awareness of God's mercy and grace, and the need to love God. So it is that the spirits of different religions come together. Beliefs and narratives about the deities may be very divergent, by contrast.

Whereas religions which concentrate on the contemplative may or may not portray similar heavens, the theistic faiths tend to do so. Naturally the imagery may sometimes be different; but the notion of living a personal life of praise and adoration, and indeed happiness, close to God in heaven is a common theme. There may also be clashes over what it is that brings you to salvation, since duties in various faiths indeed vary, as do ways of responding piously to God.

Similarly, theistic religions have traditionally believed in long or even eternal punishments. Sometimes these are thought of as purgatories in which an individual expiates or works off her or his sin, and sometimes as unremitting hells.

So far, then, we can note some possible likenesses: the contemplative experience, the numinous experience, God as Other, the importance of loving God, the possibility of a blissful heaven and of an awful purgatory or hell. Not all of these need go together: in particular you can have a mystical religion without a numinous component, or the converse, or a combination of the two, with the prospect of an experiential union between the soul and God.

Religions East and West, and in particular of South Asian and Middle Eastern origin, differ about reincarnation or rebirth. Hinduism and Buddhism in particular conceive of our lives as stretching endlessly through millenia, and taking diverse forms. Only ultimate liberation will finish the round of rebirth. It is thought that the quality of your actions will dictate the mode or level of your reincarnation, whether as an insect, an animal, a human, a god or what have you. The idea of karma, namely that our actions determine our status in future lives, does not need a God to administer it (so to speak), even though theistic systems in South Asia believe that karma comes about through the will of God.

Karma can work on its own, automatically; it becomes the mode through which our individuality expresses itself. In the case of Buddhism neither a divine creator nor a soul is necessary to explain the transitions from life to life. The psychological predisposition of a person as he fades from one life explains how it is that he is reborn in whatever form he will attain.

On the whole the West has not shared this belief. It is true that it existed in ancient Greece, and that there were tentative impulses to incorporate it into the Christian tradition. It is also true that up to 20 per cent of modern Westerners seem to believe in the idea (a little mysterious is this continuing attraction). It has its enduring logic, of course, from a number of points of view: it points to moral gradualism and gentle improvement; it provides bodily existence in different forms and so on.

Another area of overlap between traditions is in the field of ethics. Different faiths incorporate the belief that lying, killing, stealing and certain sexual relations are wrong. Of course, the content of each of these major prohibitions may vary. In some traditions all killing of animals is banned (Jainism) or discouraged (Buddhism), and not simply applying to humans only. In some, all perversions of speech are wrong, and not just telling untruths. Again in some, adultery is defined in one way and in others in another. Some traditions are internally divided: homosexuality is allowed among some Christians but thought wrong by others; polygamy is all right for some Muslims but discouraged by others; abortion is disallowed by some Jews and not by others. And so forth. Major traditions have some version of the Golden Rule: Do not do unto others what you would not have them do unto you. Ideas of brotherhood, friendship, love, compassion are normal. In general then, there is a considerable ethical agreement among faiths.

It is in the areas of myth or narrative and in the ritual dimension that the chief divergences occur. Or to put matters a little differently in regard to the former, it is over revelation that the chief gaps show. In the Hindu tradition we have deep stories about Vishnu, Shiva and the Goddess, which first of all diverge between themselves — the iconography and values of the three display different spirits. In turn, the myths of the Hindus are very different from those of the Buddhists.

The latter believe in a series of earthly Buddhas who are not gods, even if their tradition came to influence the *avatara* theory of the Hindus. In the Mahayana there are all the stories of Amitabha and Avalokitesvara and other Buddhas and Bodhisattvas, who are not pulsating creators as with the Hindu deities. In the case of China there are the stories of the immortal Lao-tzu and other divinities, all in the Taoist tradition. In the Confucian there are the soberer accounts of K'ung and the Dukes of Chou. The Chinese flavours differ greatly from the Indian ones. Meanwhile the stories of the patriarchs, prophets and kings in the Hebrew scriptures may be shared in part by Jews, Christians and Muslims, but with very different meanings. The Jews do not see Isaiah as foretelling Jesus; and the Muslims see Jesus as a prophet inferior to the Messenger of God, Muhammad. Jesus for them did not die upon the Cross.

The tendency for these groups is to dismiss stories told in other traditions as mere myths. A myth is for them a false story. Their own stories are really true, really historical. But where they dispute between their monotheistic traditions they regard the others' accounts as mere distortions (or worse, malicious fabrications). In many ways the gaps are deeper, the cleavages less resoluble, among those who claim history on their side. It is very difficult to know quite what to do about differences in revelation. We shall return to this issue later. But there might be a way to soften conflict, and that would be by taking the route of transcendental symbolism, such as the theory of Swami Vivekananda.

This route leads to saying that different revelations refer to the one Divine Reality, depicted through divergent symbols in the traditions. The village Hindu thinks of Vishnu, the village Arab of Allah, the Russian Christian of Christ and so on. There are different stories of the gods, but really only one God, transcending all the various symbols. When Vivekananda preached the unity of religions at the World's Parliament of Religion in Chicago in 1893 his message was immediately popular. It was, however, resisted by harder-line interpreters of the narratives: for the Orthodox Christian or Jew or Muslim in particular it was not acceptable. It seemed to water down the whole fact of revelation. Vivekananda's and others' attempts to soften differences could be depicted as destroying uniqueness. And so it is that though the notion of the transcendental unity of religions is attractive to some it is not so to others. It does not ultimately resolve the differences between supposed revelations: it merely adds an extra theory to those already existing. However, it is an option which, in due course, we will have to take seriously.

Still, are there not themes found in various scriptures which echo one another? There are of course, partly because the world both about us and within us is much the same. God is sun and moon; he sends down the rain and fructifies the earth; he is in the tempest and the ocean; she pushes up the shoots in spring; she revives the earth; he restores the dead after the winter; she is love; she is jealous; he is our father, she is our mother; he guards our forefathers and so on. But though such echoes resonate, they leave sharp disagreements about the nature of reality, and more about the nature of salvation.

Another dimension of religion where there are differences is in ritual. It is not so much that there are not important overlapping themes. Many religions for instance encourage or demand the practice of pilgrimage — in classical Christianity, in Islam, and in the Hindu, Buddhist and Taoist traditions. Yet it turns out that different pilgrimages are wanted. The Muslim is supposed to go to Mecca — but other people from outside the faith are banned from it. The Christian goes to Jerusalem, but to the Holy Sepulchre, not the Wailing Wall. Hindus go to Varanasi (Benares), and

Buddhists to Sarnath and Bodh-Gaya. In short, rituals formally overlap, but they also contradict each other. The Christian is liable to think the Muslim mistaken in going to Mecca, and the latter conversely thinks the Christian mistaken in identifying the truth so exclusively with such places as the Holy Sepulchre.

For the mainstream Christian the Eucharist is central, but is worse than useless from the standpoint of the Muslim. The well-meaning Hindu, such as Vivekananda, may think that it is good of the Christian to participate in symbolic acts, but he does not read necessity into the rite. So in general the divergent ritual lives, like the different revelations, are divisive.

I have so far looked at revelation as it is in books. But we could also look at it in terms of the ideal figures presented in the traditions, such as Lao-tzu, the Buddha, Krishna, Muhammad, Jesus and others. There are not necessarily conflicts here, but the ideals are surely very diverse. The nearest two are Lao-tzu and the Buddha, both living to ripe ages, preaching non-violence, offering liberation. But while the Buddha advised princes, he was not the leader in setting up a new political community as with Muhammad. Perhaps Muhammad and Moses can be compared from this angle. Rama and Krishna have a certain analogy with those two leaders. But the stories are so wildly different — Krishna disporting himself naughtily with the cowgirls, for instance (here however, he echoes a more theistic theme: the love of God for the souls of men and women — the tales not exactly to be taken literally). One might put together an anthology of magisterial and ideal utterances drawn from these great leaders. Such an anthology, however would begin to break apart, because what Jesus says about God's nature might be echoed in the Krishna legends, and yet neither can be reconciled with the message of the Buddha. And the flavour of the Qur'anic teachings diverges widely from that of the *Analects*.

Another possible way of reconciling religions might be by working an "ecumenical" linkage. That is, there are ways in which some aspects of Buddhism have resemblances to Christianity or aspects thereof. Francis Xavier jokingly remarked on arrival in Japan that Luther had gone there first (he meant of course Shinran, whose doctrine of grace was like Luther's: if a good man could be saved, how much more so a sinner?). If you can take traditions T1 and T2 and note that subtradition T1A is like subtradition T2A, though not like T2B, you can achieve in this kind of way the construction of a network of linkages between traditions. We shall have to consider later what this would show, but it is an intriguing way of reducing harsh cleavages between whole traditions. So it is that the religions which display a kind of numinous–luminous union go together, even if they may have emanated from rather diverse sources. Thus we could propose the following strands of religion to be similar:

High Mahayana ideas of union with Amitabha;
Christian medieval mysticism (and Thomas Merton and

others in this century);
Islamic Sufism, of al-Ghazali, Rumi, al-Arabi and others;
The Hindu doctrine of *bhedabhedavada* or
   identity-in-difference and analogues;
Certain aspects of Neoconfucianism, especially Wang
   Yangming;
Elements of Kabbalism and Hasidism.

This would provide linkages across some of the greatest religions, and we could add examples from Sikhism and elsewhere. This will give us something to think about when we come to our big question "Which faith?".

So far we have looked at the traditional main religions — not all of them but at least some of the major ones. We have not yet looked at the smaller and more fragmented religions, which are found in such segments of the globe as Africa, North America, South America and Australia. What of them?

First, their adherents typically believe in a High God or Spirit and beneath him or her or it there are ranged lesser deities. There is often the feeling that our concerns are too small to pin onto one Great God. If I wish to pray for my pain to ease in my stomach or knee, why should I be bothering the Lord of the Universe? A similar sentiment unites Catholic saints and the Sufi holy men. Only perhaps the Jews have that wonderful ability to bring the simply human and the awesomely divine together in a serious and also humorous combination. At any rate, many people do feel that the lesser deity is more appropriate to personal ailments than the Great God. It is, as I have said, somewhat typical for smaller-scale religions to hold together in a tension the Great Spirit and the lesser gods. You get the same thing, sometimes presented in a more systematically philosophical way, in Hinduism. It is what I call *refracted theism.*

This is the belief in gods which themselves reflect or are refracted from the One God. From a narrative and symbolic point of view they have many properties, both male and female, both local and universal, yet they are all so many versions of the One Reality. There is something of an analogy, as it happens, in Christianity. In the Catholic tradition it seems as if there are many Madonnas: the Virgin of Guadalupe, the Black Madonna of Czestochowa, the Madonna del Soccorso in Lenno, and so forth. There are different legends about the Virgin and the ways she has appeared in many different visions, and saved folk in varying ways in various places and areas. Yet they are all somehow the same Virgin. One is black, another brown, another white: but they all reflect the one Mother of God.

Well, the same phenomenon, but even more so, is to be found in the Hindu tradition, concerning the gods and the One Reality. It is a kind of theism, of the one in many. This idea is less systematically worked out in many of the smaller religions, but it exists there too. It is more systematically elaborated in the Hindu case, which has a tradition of theistic philosophy, namely various versions of the Vendanta, which states with the utmost clarity that there is One Lord.

Now, refracted theism is something which we also need to take seriously as a way of presenting what I have already also called transcendental symbolism. It opens up the possibility of different stories mapping the routes to salvation. It exhibits not a monomyth, but a polymyth, even if it points only to a monotheos, not a polytheos. Some might think it was a cheap form of theism; others would praise it as a tolerant and realistic doctrine. Later we shall have to survey grounds of choosing which interpretation is, after all, better.

So far we have been sketching certain points of agreement which are possible between the religions of the world. But we need also at least to glance at secular worldviews. For it may turn out that religions need to blend with one or more of them. Are there points at which such worldviews themselves overlap with traditional religions or with some sub-traditions of them?

It is notable that a major strand in modern (mainly Western) thinking is a kind of liberal individualism, going back to the Enlightenment and to nineteenth century utilitarianism. Such a philosophy stresses the rights of individuals and the basis of morality in the creation of human happiness for the greatest number, and the minimization of suffering or unhappiness for as many as possible. Notoriously there are difficulties both in defining and in quantifying suffering and happiness. Still, we can see analogues and affinities between such individualistic forms of humanism and some traditional value-systems. We have noted that the radical tradition of Protestantism already has a strongly individualistic strand. It may in some respects have an otherworldly view of human welfare and illfare. Even so it is participat- ory in the world, and has laid some of the valuational basis of modern capitalism. The latter has to do with individualism for various reasons.

First, it has a cold view of individuals, but nevertheless an influential one: that is, capitalism in general does not care whether an individual is male or female, black or white. It is true that it may use social prejudices to exploit individuals, say women — but not out of its own ideological bias. Prejudice against women is more likely in a highly traditional society than in a newly capitalist one. Second, capitalism has some interest in a liberal, that is an open, society. Polycentricity is of its essence, and it is against older forms of centralism, and even more against modern, mainly Marxist, varieties of the centralist State. So there is a natural symbiosis between capitalism and liberalism. Still, the relations between capitalism and the open society are by no means always clear. Some forms of capitalism, say in South Korea, have developed under authoritarian regimes, as also in Chile. But in the long run I would argue that the open society wins under capitalism.

In turn, the open society favours things which capitalism cherishes, such as the development of science and technology, which are important also in human understanding. More generally, it favours criticism within society: we humans need it if we are to avoid the absurdities of dogmatism and the cruelties of arrogance. Because of the importance of openness, the qualities which rulers and leaders exhibit are of the greatest importance. It was one of the great virtues of Confucianism that K'ung saw the importance of the virtues of the elite. But we need the virtues of the open society, doubtless, beyond the elite: humility, objectivity, empathy and so on are important for all of us. At any rate, individualism and the open society do chime in with certain varieties of radical Protestantism. But they also chime in with some other strands of traditional religion — with Theravada religion, for instance. On the other hand, individualism is somewhat inimical to later modern Hinduism, with older Confucianism, and with relatively small-scale traditionalism. Nor does it chime in with the ethos of Marxism: the latter emphasizes egalitarian and social justice (but so does social democracy in the Scandinavian mode), but neglects the rights and meaning of the individual. It also calls itself scientific but does not practise the openness of science. So in brief, there is a kind of alliance between openness, democracy, individualism, science and truth. It seems to me most likely that these values (products of our modern age for the most part) need to be melded with those of Christianity or whatever religion you happen to favour. In short, liberal individualism is not at all irrelevant to the values of religion, or to the values of a new synthesis between religion and social action. We all visit, so to speak, at the blades of the liberal grass.

The reason why Buddhism is individualist is partly because of rebirth: your present life is your own responsibility from previous births. Now, though the same is true in Hinduism and Sikhism, and in other religions holding to reincarnation; the Hindu tradition has, also, a heavy view of collectivity, because of the caste system, itself cemented — in a manner of speaking — with the sticky substance of ritual duties. Similarly, Confucianism has a rather heavy view of social obligations. Then we have nationalism entering the scene, so that social obligations come to equal national obligations.

For instance, Japanese solidarity is deeply felt and reinforced by a multitude of ritual obligations. Even today, with the Emperor no longer held officially to be divine, homage to the Emperor helps to keep the people together and is fading only slowly. In its present form such homage is a weakened version of what was customary pre-World War II. Nevertheless, it contains many deep echoes from the Meiji period, when the Emperor came to be treated as a special link in the chain of patriotic feelings.

Since liberal individualism is much associated with modernism, and goes with a critical stance towards claims and theories and values, it is something ineluctable for modern versions of religion. If fundamentalism and analogous developments represent a kind of backlash against modernism, this is only part of the truth. In different cultures and traditions, fundamentalism represents a similar investment in individualism through the thought that personal salvation comes from a sort of conversion. There are plenty of born-again Muslims in the universities of Egypt, and newly invigorated students in the Hindu revivalism of today. The fundamentalists of America look back to an age when family values were not in such disarray. The common link is conversion — it is individual feeling.

By contrast Marxism, though it has a critical aspect, is collectivist in spirit. It borrows its eschatological myth in effect from Christianity, though it makes the consummation of history distinctly this-worldly. Its claim to be scientific is based on a view of history which purports to be scientific but which itself cannot be verified in any strictly scientific way. It is typically very hostile to traditional religions, and has ground them down, or attempted to do so wherever it has attained political power, from Vietnam to Russia and from Uzbekistan to Cuba. Even so, there has been, in Liberation Theology (a Catholic reforming movement in Latin America and elsewhere), an attempt to blend traditional religious and Marxist values. Since governments in much of the previously Marxist world have collapsed, Marxism is less of a serious option today and survives most vigorously in its social democratic form, itself a blend of socialism and individualism.

In brief, the secular ideologies, notably liberal individualism, may be blended with traditional religions (themselves suitably modified). In choosing a faith it is important to incorporate into one's values those ideas which are ineluctable in the pursuit of modern knowledge and practical living. It happens that scientific and other forms of discovery and insight themselves seem to depend on the open society, which provides the possibility of criticizing former theories and social practices. The open society has to protect the individual and encourage creativity. From this point of view it seems important to blend religious tradition with liberalism.

This however does not mean that there cannot be critiques of certain interpretations of individualism. Very often a utilitarian ethic is based on the shallowest ideas of happiness. Traditional religions, in part because of their dependence on religious experience, have deeper views of happiness and suffering, and may bring these to bear in analyzing and shaping human life.

We have seen in this chapter that there are overlaps between religions. They have their conflicts on the details of revelation and ritual; but they have their coincidences of values in various ways. It would seem to be sensible to view the question of "Which faith?" in the light of such agreements. More, it is useful for us to reflect upon them when we consider whether we can evolve anything like a global ethos. I now move on to consider how we might begin to judge ideas and teachers.

CHAPTER FOUR

JUDGING IDEAS AND TEACHERS

We have already seen how religion is linked to experience, living ritual and ethics. It is not just a theoretical matter. We often admire people for living what they believe; sincerity and seriousness count, from this point of view, more than truth. Yet on the other hand, what if a person sincerely practises what is mistaken or evil? There was little doubt that Hitler was sincere in his ideology, but that did not justify the terrible course of his life, or the path down which he led the German people.

The importance of living one's ideas is mainly that, if you are both sincere and successful, when they are good ones, they yield wonderful fruits. Buddhists say that in matters of speech you should if possible utter what is true, useful and pleasant. So one might say with lives and actions — they should be useful and pleasant and based somehow on truth, or on realism.

Training can be important in all this. The idea of moral training is that it enables the individual to take control over her life and direct it towards ethical channels. Similarly spiritual experience does not just come all of a sudden out of nowhere, but can in part depend on the circumstances. Very often, these involve the sincere application of a person to her path. Consequently we have organizations, ranging from psychoanalytic practices to Sufi brotherhoods, and from the Buddhist Sangha to guru traditions, which present possibilities for spiritual instruction and training. Very often the idea of truth links with that of the spiritual instructor. This throws the onus back to those whom in general terms we can call gurus, whether they belong to orders or brotherhoods or simply to a loose tradition of laying down the spiritual law. How do we judge these persons: are they sincere, are they insightful, do they have the truth? How do we tell? There are two directions from which they can be approached. From one angle, we can ask whether they seem profound and are kind, whether they are rich (in itself a bad sign), whether their authority masks vanity, whether they are banal. From that angle we estimate their characters. Their power may corrupt them, or not, and it is relevant to know.

? same as "profound" or "banal".

But from another angle, we may judge them by what they say and teach. Is it rational? Is it relevant? Is it compatible with what we know already? Here we are more directly concerned with matters of truth. Of course, especially in religion and worldviews these things are not easy to judge. Still, it is wise for us not to be too overwhelmed by gurus and to try and judge for ourselves. This is a matter too of judging not just individuals as teachers, but also collectivities as gurus—such as the Catholic Church, or the Theravadin tradition, or Iranian Ayatollahs, or the Church of Scotland. There is perhaps a paradox here, which we need to deal with at the outset because it has such widespread ramifications, in relation not only to organizations but in general to all claims to revelation.

Claims to authority

Many years ago I was taken by a spiritually rather radical Catholic priest in Bombay — he a Goanese Catholic — to visit a guru whom he admired, who ran a statistical advisory bureau in Bombay and lived in an apartment on Melabar Hill, an elegant enough part of the city. He was a Parsee except that he thought himself a Hindu. When we reached his home, there he was at the end of a long room, with disciples, mainly Hindus, arranged down the walls. We sat near the end opposite the guru. He spoke on, and I sat there like a sore thumb, being the only Westerner. At a certain point glaring somewhat at me, the guru said that the East was spiritual and the West material — a common cliché. I decided to interrupt him, and asked him what he thought about my action in going into a record store and buying a record of a late Beethoven quartet. Was this a spiritual act or a material one, or both, or neither? After a moment's startlement he chuckled and said "Good, you want to have an argument. None of these people," he said scanning his unfortunate disciples, "ever want to argue back!" (Poor buggers, I thought.) But if he was willing to argue, he was coming down to my level. Where was the authority? Well, he mentioned spiritual experience.

Supposing a person cites her or his religious experience as authority, what do we do about it? It is of course in general like saying "I saw it happen". But there are still some nagging doubts. The criteria of seeing are not quite so precise. (Consider the problems of judging eye-witnesses in daily life.) The validity of religious experiences is very much more culture-prone. More, there are those who do not acknowledge their validity at all. Let us look first into this syndrome — of those who regard them as mere projections, delusions, hallucinations or the like.

The main reason for distrust of religious experience is varieties of projection theory, ranging from Feuerbach, through Marx, to Freud. But this reason itself is not well founded, even if it be not without foundation. It is not well founded for various reasons. First, each is based on a philosophy: in Feuerbach's case a kind of Hegelianism; in Marx's a kind of materialism; in Freud's another kind of materialism. All are themselves fraught with problems. Each is open to the accusation of its own kind of projection. Let us take Marx as the most egregious example. Think how many intellectuals, under the spell of Marx, projected their values onto Moscow,

Beijing and Tirana. Think how many illusions were thrown on the screen of history in the name of Marxist theory.

Second come the different projection theories and their particular illusions of history. We can see this most clearly in the case of Freud. In his *Moses and Monotheism* Freud made up the most egregious bit of ancient history, which no scientific historian of religion could take seriously. Third, the projection theorists did not take seriously enough the essential softness of philosophical criteria. Feuerbach could accept a kind of idealism to underpin his theory (itself, by the way, mainly oriented towards Christianity), but did not seem to realize the essential subjectivity of so much philosophy. There will be more on this later. As if the previous three objections were not bad enough, there is the fact that all three thinkers were terribly ignorant of other traditions. How can you judge religion as a whole from a critique of only one of its traditions (or two if you include Judaism, as with Freud)? Can you generalize from the family life of Vienna? How does the Oedipus complex work in Sri Lanka, with no father figure? Future generations will, I believe, look back on theories such as those of Hegel, Marx and Freud and shake their heads at the ability of our intellectuals to believe myths with such notoriously fragile bases, and which are themselves such obvious – dare I say it – projections?

The history of the epoch from World War II till the collapse of the Soviet Union is in many ways depressing. Our intellectuals in the West have been highly intelligent idiots, often enough: uncritical in an age of science and rationality, and treasonable clerks in an age of openness of enquiry. Even those who have stood up for human values have bought the materialist hypothesis often enough. Democrats themselves have been willing to buy into a suppression of worldviews other than their own, and to despise religion while respecting amazingly speculative mythologies. Enough, however, of this intemperate aside. I justify it to indicate that different value-systems should at least be treated with equality.

But to return to the issue of religious experience. There are of course reasons to be suspicious despite what I have said against projectionists. The numinous experience, the contemplative path, cosmic feelings and shamanism are not exactly everyone's cup of tea. On the other hand, there is no doubt from empirical research that there are many more people who undergo dramatic religious experiences than had previously been thought. The reason is simple: in the old days (that is until recently) it was common in Western cultures for such effusions about religion to be despised. Claims to have seen God were distinctly unfashionable. They could land you in a mental hospital. Nowhere has worldview conformism perhaps been more rigorously exercised than in the psychiatric profession, itself greatly subject to conformist training. Anyway, it was not fashionable to claim a numinous encounter. It is not much less unfashionable to claim a contemplative insight.

Nevertheless, if a person appeals to her religious experience we have to take that seriously. Even if the general climate of scepticism (which despite my strictures above I regard as not altogether unjustified) means that we need to enter a query about it, it is nevertheless relevant to try to base one's pronouncements on direct experience.

What then do we make of such appeals? I wish here to make a distinction between two types. One is where a person says she thought she saw God or attained enlightenment. That is one variety. The other we may think of as holistic — where a person claims a whole purchase on the truth. Not just a conversion, but to a particular and detailed web of truth, such as Islam or the Baptist persuasion.

The thought that one has seen the Lord, or the Truth or nirvana is less specific than the idea that one is converted. The one is a more impressive claim, the other a greater one; the one works in a cross-cultural context more easily; the other in a home context, where people are not used to alternatives. Since we can point to similar conversions in different cultural and religious contexts it is reasonable to favour the lesser claims to the more network-like. This is not to denigrate or downplay the conversion experience: it is merely to say that, profound as it may be, it proves less than the converted person thinks it does. It may be quite valid and yet less probative than is claimed. The reasons are obvious. It used to be said "Never trust a god over thirty": we could instead say "Never trust a testimony that is too detailed". Trust the feeling, but not the conclusion. The very facts of the similarity of religious experiences in different traditions surely point to our human affinities, and these point away from detailed divisions.

There is a large underlying question here, and that is about the status of the sacred book. It is true that in some traditions the sacred text is not strictly a book: for instance in the Hindu tradition the Veda is an oral tradition, and the beginnings of the Buddhist canon were spoken — recited text handled by expert reciters. But still, many traditions did produce books: the Hebrew scriptures, the New Testament, the Qur'an, the Chinese classics, the Taoist Canon, the Buddhist Canon, and so on. Typically, what was counted as revelation was a book or set of books. One of the most remarkable of human artefacts came to be the locus for divine self-disclosure. Why should this be? And how should you choose between them? Perhaps the most telling of all titles is the Sikh *Guru Granth* — the Teacher Book.

There has been a large clash between traditional ways of looking at holy books as integral presentations, and modern ways, probing their composition. It is of course an open assumption of Biblical scholarship that you can look for the different strands that go to make up a given text such as a Gospel. This makes it hard to cleave to a "fundamentalist" interpretation. A better case, perhaps, is an integral interpretation of the Qur'an, since in principle all the bits of the texts were revealed to and through the same person, God's Prophet. The very fact that the Qur'an happened during a life time, in fact a small section of a life time, sets it apart from the Hebrew scriptures, made up of parts composed over several hundred years. There is also a large time span covering early *sruti* or primary revelation in the Hindu tradition, through to later *smrti* or secondary revelation. Similarly there is a large enough stretch covering the materials in the *Guru Granth*. And so on.

I would argue that being fundamentalist cuts you off from the mainstream of modern thinking and of the practice of the humanities and social sciences. I think this is too high a price to pay. It runs parallel to being cut off from modern science. This, of course, is not at all to say that all scientific theories have to be swallowed. The fact is that a great many serious errors have been made in science. By fundamentalism, I am thinking here in particular of that kind of interpretation of the Bible which rejects swathes of scientific conclusions, for example about the relatively long time between the "beginning" of the cosmos and the present age. There need in principle be no conflict between scriptures and scientific knowledge.

There does not seem to be, on the face of it, any necessary clash between the Qur'an and modern cosmology. Even rather "hard" interpreters of scripture may leave room for metaphors and analogies, rather than literal meanings. Still, if a scripture is in fact interpreted to clash with well-established theses in science, this is serious. It is a serious sign of the falsity of the interpretation in question. In short I would advocate a certain "modernism" as indicative of truth. Yet modernism is not so much a creation of a particular faith as something which emerged in this century and the last, initially in the West, and which is found in different forms in diverse faiths.

Let me not be misunderstood. Though it looks as if those who deny scientific conclusions on the basis of a particular scriptural interpretation are likely to be wrong, and to be holding and maybe preaching a false worldview, it does not mean that by affirming this we need to fail to respect those who hold the supposedly false view. There may be some good fruits of their position and in any case, in an open and liberal milieu, toleration and respect should prevail. If I introduce some measure of liberalism as a criterion of truth, the reason is a straightforward one. It appears that the open society is a necessary condition of scientific and other forms of discovery. If we sacrifice openness we shall sacrifice all the great intellectual and scientific advances of the human race. While there may be something noble and heroic about communities that withdraw into a holy ignorance, they do not represent a reasonable choice of faith. No doubt they would not be at all persuaded by reading this book! No doubt by the very nature of the probable readership, my plea for "modernist" religion involves preaching to the converted. We can summarize by saying that a flexible attitude to "revealed" tradition is important.

But this still leaves the problem of how we can possibly choose one tradition of given scriptural injunctions over another. If there is the hint of an answer it lies in fruits — both moral and spiritual. We shall later have something more particular to say on the ethical side. Regarding spiritual fruits, it is worth noting that the most successful religions have tended to shape civilizations and whole societies. If you are born within such a tradition, it is of course not something to despise. Rather something which may have its irksome aspects but will also have created a way of life which in principle is worth continuing, preserving and adapting.

Much of the problem of religions in the modern world concerns the need to change in the face of social and cultural developments. So while loyalty to a tradition does not at all preclude changes — on the contrary it demands them — yet it recognizes the creative aspects of the past. It is possible to "fill out" traditions, and make them more inclusive. Such adaptations relate to some criteria of spiritual truth. For since there is more than one variety, as we have seen, of religious or spiritual experience, and it is hard to favour one over the other, it would appear reasonable that we should favour traditions that embrace both major types.

For example, both classical Islam and the Christian Catholic tradition have embraced both the religion of worship and with it the numinous experience and the mystical or contemplative path with its experience of the purification of consciousness. These are fuller manifestations of spiritual awareness than that provided by traditional Calvinism and traditional Theravada Buddhism. Yet Calvinism, somewhat narrow in its spiritual scope, nevertheless favours a wide role for education, sometimes missing in the classical Catholic ordered society. There is no reason though why other traditions should not take over the admirable Calvinist educational drive. There is no reason why Calvinism should not begin to experiment with the monastic life (nutritive of the experience of higher yogic consciousness).

So far I have pictured two criteria: one is a liberal ethos, and the second is richness of religious experience and the attendant practice. I have simplified the criteria regarding experience by supposing it to fall into two main forms: the numinous or prophetic and the mystical or contemplative. From this perspective, one would be less attracted to modern reforming and revivalist Islamic movements, which tend to be very critical of the Sufi movement. But actually in its heyday Sufism provided that strong injection of the contemplative life which might be lacking in orthodox Islam.

There is another kind of spirituality which is less easy to evaluate. This is the kind which arises from living the narratives of scripture, or following the patterns of chief figures in the narrative. For instance, a notable part of the Biblical revival after the Protestant Reformation was the way people used reflection on Biblical readings to order their daily lives and feelings. There are analogues in the idea of the chosen deity in the Hindu tradition: here a believer follows the example of Rama or Krishna, or whoever he is specially devoted to. There is in Islam the imitation of the virtues of the Prophet and his religious example, and these are manifested through the complex of traditions about his life. How does one choose between the disparate heroes of the traditions: the Son in Christianity, the Prophet in Islam, the famous rabbis in Judaism, the sages in Confucianism, the varied masters, avatars, mystics and so on in other traditions?

Here openness might be a criterion. It might seem reasonable and sensitive for a religion to be open to learning from others. Of course, traditional faiths have sometimes been "jealous". They have often claimed a unique and whole grasp of the truth. But I have argued that there can be no certainty in such a claim and it may appear arrogant to suppose that there is nothing that can be learned from outside a given tradition or sub-tradition. If we were to accept openness as a test, then it would rule in favour of those manifestations of a tradition that were willing to learn from others and to recognize others' share of spiritual potency. So then the Christian or the Jew or the Hindu could learn from the ideal of the sage, for example. The Sufi could learn from the yogin. The guru could learn from Christ's example. From this angle, ecumenical Christianity, Sufism and the modern Hindu tradition would be attractive, as would much of Buddhism (which in a whole civilizational experiment managed eventually to coexist fruitfully with both Taoism and Confucianism, together with localized religious activities, in pre-modern China).

There is a dialectic of course in such matters. There tend to be backlashes against such easy-going outwardness, which strikes many people as a threat to the integrity of the faith. The problem is how to hang on to the essentials (whatever they are). Although a Christian might learn from Confucius or Ramanuja, she will not want to let go of her feel for the centrality of Christ. The Sufi who takes on board some of the insights of the yogis does not wish to lose his loyalty to the Prophet and his message. So openness has to be accompanied by a kind of "essentialism" on which to anchor faith. It seems desirable that a faith should be liberal, spiritually comprehensive and open to the insights of others. If others wish to react against this and affirm an inward-looking integralism, so be it. The more expansive view makes much more sense in the modern global environment.

It should be noted here, though, that there is a certain serendipity and conditionality about choices. I pass to this topic, briefly.

The importance of situations

A person's choice of sub-tradition or of tradition may to an extent be dictated by circumstances. For instance, until Vatican II (1962-65), when the Catholic Church underwent profound reforms under the stimulus of Pope John XXIII, there was little modernism or liberalism in the official line of the Roman Church. It had striven since the late nineteenth century to suppress impulses towards the open Biblical scholarship which had flourished among certain of the Protestant Churches, notably in Germany, Britain and the United States. Also, other liberal ideas, such as those associated with the new nationalisms of Europe, and self-criticism of the institution, were hardly encouraged. In those days the Church did not meet the first criterion I listed above. But after Vatican II everything changed. Moreover, society had altered. There was no feeling any more that the Church could seriously exercise much coercion within the democracies. Remaining Catholic had become voluntary. In effect, loyalty to the Pope came to be a matter of choice. Hence his pronouncements are no longer greeted with automatic respect and agreement. Thus it is that Catholic Italy has the lowest birth-rate in the world. So in the last quarter of a century an Anglican for example, valuing her freedom, might be tempted to enter the Roman Church, on the ground that not only has it the liberal ethos, but it continues a treasury of Orders and forms of the contemplative and socially caring life. Or that person might work instead on behalf of closer relations between the sub-traditions.

Again, a Muslim might be looking at the still unsatisfactory state of Islamic life in the contemporary world. A once great civilization is fragmented by nationalism, dominated in places by postcolonial forces, unable fully to integrate modern living and traditional values, and so on. In these circumstances he might reason that there were more vital matters than stimulating a resurgence of Sufism (even if Sufi thought copes well with science and helps to express a deep personal spirituality). So conditionally, in view of the circumstances of today, such a Muslim might lend his loyalty to an integralist movement. But were such 'fundamentalist' forces ever able to repair the fabric of Islam, then there might be a different direction to his thinking.

Again, a Theravada Buddhist might feel that, in many ways, Mahayana Buddhism is more open than the Theravada in the present epoch, and has a wider range of spirituality, and is also not so involved in past conflicts with Tamils. In these circumstances he might move in the direction of the Greater Vehicle, emphasizing previous Mahayana influences upon Sinhala society.

Another factor is how we may view our heritages. A Catholic Christian might not think herself as likely to have ever become an Anabaptist, but might be glad that the Anabaptists had played so notable a part in Protestant history, since they were notable contributors to the formation of modern individualism, which in turn has been the principal soil out of which feminism has grown. They were not the only contributors, of course, to individualism, but still important. So such a Catholic while not being disloyal to her tradition could well in retrospect be highly appreciative of former anti-Catholic movements and their role in reform. In brief, given circumstances may dictate our actual choices and past judgements.

Narratives and rituals as appealing

We have so far made some appeal to richness of religious experience. We have noted briefly too how a certain kind of spirituality may be shaped by the imitation of great figures, or the attempt to apply passages from the past revelatory tradition to one's own life. How the narratives appeal is partly a matter of their deeper lessons but, about which lesson is more profound, there can easily be, and is, disagreement.

For example, the narrative of Jesus' suffering and death is something which means a great deal to most Christians. It has embedded in it various messages. One could be put as follows: God, in creating a world in which suffering was bound to follow the arising of free creatures who could respond in liberty and love to the self-revelation of the Divine Being, already knew and was committed to sharing in that human world, and undergoing the suffering which is the lot of creatures. In short, there is a special response in the Christian faith to the problem of evil and suffering. The death of Christ also reverberates with earlier images of sacrifice: he becomes an expiatory offering for human error, etc.

Now, though the notion of incarnation is well developed in the Hindu tradition, the deeper messages are different. Sacrifice (oddly, considering the traditional Brahmin preoccupation with it) does not play such a central conceptual role in the lives and work of Rama and Krishna. But Krishna's amours and Rama's love of Sita are figures signifying the fascination of God as divine lover, and so on.

The narrative significance of the history of Israel and its readying itself to become the basis of the wider Jewish religion is different, for it deals with community and communal relations with the Divine. It seems therefore as if diverse narratives are bound to give rise to different spiritualities. The message for the Jewish people is, in part at least, that by their example and suffering they can lead the world forward as part of the divine plan. But how can we measure this message against other ones?

As I have remarked, judgement in these matters is somewhat aesthetic. Here a person is more likely to be attracted in one way rather than another. It is not a matter of cool choice, and it may be that a person feels chosen, rather than themselves doing the choosing.

It is also as if the person pondering different revelations reflects that they help to define different communities: and so more broadly than the narratives that help to define them, there are the characteristics of the communities — their styles, which constitute the embodiment of the revealed narrative. It is this embodied narrative with which the individual may or may not fall in love. It is hard to see how we can rate one narrative more "true" than another. Yet it is ironic that they have to be deemed true in some sense or another in order to work.

The fact is, of course, that the different communities will continue to exist in the world indefinitely. It is scarcely conceivable that one worldview will come to conquer the world, unless it be some global ideology that nevertheless finds a place for the major ideologies and traditions. And so in choosing a community a person needs to be guided by an aesthetic sense of what is spiritually right for her.

Similar remarks apply to the appeal or otherwise of rituals. There is no doubt that some faiths are remarkably effective from a ritual angle: for instance, public worship in Islamic countries is highly impressive in the way it expresses and reinforces a strong sense of the divine power and presence. Again, Buddhist prescriptions on the practice of meditation seem to be efficient in generating higher states of consciousness.

Clearly one aspect of a set of religious rituals or practices is whether they work. It is not much good taking communion each week if nothing changes. So part of "By their fruits ye shall know them" is whether they do what is claimed of them.

So far we have looked at various criteria. Let me list them at this point —

modernism;
richness of spiritual experience;
openness to other traditions;
attractiveness of narrative and ritual offerings;
situational relevance (both personal and social-historical);
effectiveness.

Since so far I have been discussing matters largely in relation to existing traditions, I shall add a few remarks here about secular ideologies, with special reference to scientific humanism and Marxism, as well as nationalisms.

Secular ideologies: how do they rate as compared with religions?

Scientific humanism in most of its forms rejects religious tradition. It means "humanism" in a negative way, concentrating on human rather than transcendental values. Now I shall be mentioning some of the ethical criteria in the next chapter, and so shall leave these aside here.

Scientific humanism, born in the West, has often subscribed to a narrative of history which concedes an ineluctable conflict between science and religion. While there are forms of religion, typically non-modernist ones, where such a struggle does exist, the conflict is not ineluctable. Moreover, there are some features of traditional religion which have favoured a scientific outlook. For instance, belief in a rational Creator favours the attempt to unravel the mind of God by figuring out the way in which the cosmos works; again, the Buddhist philosophy of events is close to modern scientific thinking, and more forward-looking than the theory of substances that has dominated the West since Aristotle and before.

Scientific humanism tends to ignore religious experiences (though it need not do so). The contemplative life could in principle be combined with humanistic values, if mystical states were considered sufficiently important. I am not sure, therefore, whether our list of criteria would not work well enough here too.

The case of Marxism is somewhat different, owing to its usual hostility to religions, which renders it similar to evangelical or radical versions of some religious traditions. It has its mythic narrative, which relates to the way history unfolds dialectically, moving towards the ultimate classless society. Unfortunately, its narrative has not stood up to the facts, and the recent discrediting of actual Marxist experiments in civilization point to a vast hollowness in the societies unfortunate enough to come under the aegis of the ideology. Even so one could say that the trouble with idealistic Marxism is that it has never been tried!

With such secular ideologies there is also the myth that, somehow, human kind is heading, in the manner sketched by Auguste Comte (not to mention Ludwig Feuerbach), towards a condition in which it rids itself of religion and religions. This does not seem to be happening. Even among those in the West who have shed formal adherence to a spiritual community, there remains a strong attachment to a variety of spiritual themes in life. Individuals increasingly invent their own religions.

As for nationalism, it has been the most vital mobilizing force in the modern world, at least from the French Revolution onwards. It has bound peoples in new attachments of loyalty. It has become the primary signature of identity. It has often commanded legions to die in battle, and citizens to sacrifice large sums in order to pay for warfare or its threat. It has also often blended with traditional religion to create a potent mixture of sacred patriotism. At its extreme it nourishes the politics of fascism. It has scarred the burnt face of the twentieth century in world wars and other gigantic and bitter conflicts. It rivals religion in its demands on human obedience. But, despite its ultimate demands, it does not have ultimate authority over human life. Nevertheless many men and women have fallen under its spell and given their lives in service to the nation.

Some degree of rationality called for

Hitherto we have looked at various criteria, including spiritual fruits, openness and so on. The secular ideologies often think of themselves as especially reasonable or rational. But as I have already indicated, conclusions about such matters are subject to "maybe". Still, a person should strive to fit her beliefs into a coherent or consistent framework. She should be prepared to argue for her commitment. Such rationality should take cognizance of the following areas of reflection:

First, though one or two of the classical arguments for the existence of God do not work very well, there are versions of the Cosmological Argument that have a certain, though not overwhelming, persuasiveness. (Namely the notion that there might not have been any cosmos, but nothing. So something distinct from the cosmos may be required to explain its coming into being.)

Second, it is important in the present age to reflect on the other religions from whatever angle of vision one comes at them. Do they represent partial insights into the nature of the ultimate? Do they embody the same kinds of spiritual experience as does one's own tradition? Can one's tradition find a coherent story of why the other faiths exist? To keep each other honest? To provide spiritual variety in the world?

Third, is it possible in the light of modern knowledge and today's global perspective, to retell the history of one's own tradition in such a way as to make sense of its various contributions, while not glossing over its weaknesses and errors in the past? Obviously some of this material will overlap with what I have listed elsewhere as "modernism".

But it is also vital for us to see, when we reflect about religion, that we should not be too abstract and cerebral. After all, the fruits of faiths are human beings. It is through admiration of individuals who live the faith that we are most likely to see its meaning and impact.

Since we are rarely in a position to know too many of the faithful of different traditions, even in such multicultural places as Los Angeles, London and Moscow, we have to take a lot of judgements on trust. Moreover, we probably need some philosophy which has at least some global overview, which fits our endeavours into the world scene and the unfolding of world history. Here again, I appeal to circumstances. We live in a particular epoch, where the questions asked in this book are making themselves heard. These modern (some would say post-modern) circumstances nudge us ever more urgently towards thinking like global citizens. I shall address some of the issues in the last two chapters. In the next one, I shall address more directly the issue of good and bad features of religions in the past. In other words I shall be concerned with ethical criteria and their impact on the global situation as well as on personal life.

CHAPTER FIVE

BY THEIR MORAL AND SOCIAL FRUITS

Here we address more directly the question: what can we make of the different traditions — major and other — by reference to their maxims and moral fruits? The latter of course include social and political fruits too. Naturally, since there are serious divisions of opinion about what is right and wrong, I do not pretend that the way forward in relation to criteria of excellence is clear. Fruits can vary in flavour according to the background out of which they emerge. We are not always matching like with like. Far from it.

But I would like to begin with some observations about the contemporary situation and the urgent priorities which confront us worldwide. First, the question of communal and more generally ethnic violence is particularly serious, and not only because the binding together of the globe into a single web of interactions implies that conflict in any one place will tend to have a universal impact. It happens that as I write this (April, 1994) there are serious disturbances and slaughter in Rwanda, which threaten to spill over into neighbouring Burundi. Such events are ghastly: but two hundred years ago they might have gone totally unnoticed. How long would news in those days have taken to reach Paris or Brussels? Maybe months. Maybe it would never have arrived. But now it is of active concern to the United Nations and France and Belgium.

Second, our global condition raises new questions about violence. Our technological advances have brought clever new weapons, from the fantastically effective mechanization of firearms to the development of rocketry and, above all, the creation of nuclear weapons. Violence can now be so much more lethal. We see it in daily reports of mass shootings, whether in Los Angeles or Hebron or Kashmir. We dread the day when some rogue nation or gangster organization will threaten to use a nuclear bomb. Frankly, it is not easy to be sanguine on this front, because so many ethnic and other injustices have created many sour and fanatical people, and because criminality is growing in scale.

Next there is the issue of resources. The increase in world population is getting to be alarming, particularly when it is combined with the demands of justice. As soon as poorer countries begin to get richer they place growing strains upon the world's environment. The wonderful achievements of many northern countries in fashioning a rich life for most of their citizens are, of course, looked on with envy and the world's billions want equal or more equitable shares.

It is in the light of these as well as more traditional problems of human ethics that we have to judge the traditions.

Now there is, of course, a considerable overlap of values in the various faiths. Such values as love, benevolence, compassion, mercy, and humanness are ascribed to the Divine or to the sage and saint. There are also different, but not alien, conceptions of justice. But the devil is in the detail. How can you reconcile traditional Islamic law on marriage with Christian monogamy? How can you not notice the difference between Hindu *dharma*, with its recognition of diverse classes and castes, and Quaker egalitarianism? And the heavy Confucian emphasis on *li* or appropriate ceremonial behaviour is not matched exactly in the Buddhist interpretation of ethics. And so on.

There are subtly divergent attitudes to sex — in the religions — Jewish, Christian, Islamic, Buddhist and so on. And in the modern period there have been various reactions to the use of artificial means of birth control and to homosexuality. An interesting development in respect of these issues is that doctrinal differences are now tending to emerge between different wings of the religions rather than between the religions *per se*. For example, the acceptance of birth control divides Christians, Jews and Muslims internally.

The chief ethical criteria

I shall propose here that the chief criteria of a religious movement's ethical excellence are the two main ones I have mentioned above as being of global significance — in other words the minimization of violence and the preservation of resources — together with a third, namely toleration. For in a crowded world it is necessary to give differences of opinion room to move and breathe, and to give diversities of culture the soil to bloom and flourish. As I have indicated, the application of such criteria may not lead to divergences between religions as such, nor even between denominations, but to "wings" or emphases within them (an example is that the liberal wing of Catholicism endorses artificial means of birth control). Once we have made some progress in regard to these major issues of a global character, we can use the space and calm provided to devote ourselves to spiritual deepening and training. For we should not lose sight of the fact that religions and worldviews are not merely props for utilitarian ethics, but provide patterns and shapes for living a more profound life. Let me comment a little on this before saying something more concrete about the application of the above-mentioned criteria.

There is always something to be learned about the mythic and philosophical diagnoses a religion has for the predicament of the human race. As part of the so-called 'problem of evil' we surely note that human life is far from ideal: and yet unlike the other animals, so far as we know them, we as a species are capable of vision. The cat has no eschatology, nor the flamingo its prophets. So we, with vision, look forward and back to a far better human condition. In a number of African and other myths, there is the story of how the primeval human pair somehow became alienated from God, often through reaching for an immortality that only belongs to the Divine. This often links with the idea that our ultimate salvation or immortality comes only from God. In Christianity a somewhat analogous myth translates into the doctrine of Original Sin. It is as if our lives are poisoned by the inheritance of an act of disobedience and hubris. Our wills are somehow vitiated without God's grace. We need the guidance of the Divine and of the sacred community. Because God lies outside the realm of humanity (even if She may guide us as the Spirit from within), this need to rely on the Transcendent should give us both courage and independence.

Such myths provide one model of human nature. This model contrasts with the vision of Mencius and many other Confucians, of the essential goodness of human nature. It differs too from the intermediate emphasis of much of the Jewish heritage, on the coexistence of both good and bad impulses within us. Then again, there is the more analytic, less mythic, theory of the Buddhists, that we are capable of overcoming the obstacles to nirvana — greed, hatred and delusion. This theory places much more emphasis on spiritual confusion or ignorance. It may be that we ought to test out these diagnoses more empirically. I would consider a synthesis to be possible. The Buddhist analysis seems realistic, in breaking 'sin' down into greed, hatred and delusion.

It is as if we as human animals have built a kind of egoism which craves community (and with that, hatred of outsiders) and we suffer from an illusion self-sufficiency born from belief in the reality of the ego itself. Such mythic and analytic diagnoses of the sources of human trouble are worth pondering, and in an open environment could well, as I have suggested, be synthesized.

There are of course deeper implications, beyond the ethical. Perhaps original sin does demand divine expiatory sacrifice, while greed, hatred and delusion may need resolute self-pacification and insight. In either case there is a postulated supreme happiness — regained closeness to the Divine Being, or else nirvana. It may be noted by the way, that religions tend to have a deep notion of happiness. Utilitarians in the modern philosophical tradition are admirably empirical in talking of pleasure and pain, but they need a more profound sense of the meaning of happiness to make utilitarianism plausible.

Violence and related matters

Let us, however, return from this excursion to a consideration of the three major criteria I have proposed. They tend no doubt to work synergistically: a liberal and open form of the faith is more likely to be tolerant; it is also likely to be less violent in disposition, and flexible in adapting to modern concerns with the environment. But we should not assume this is so without question. It was after all a liberal ethos which pervaded American society when it unleashed a terrible technological war in Vietnam. And very "fundamentalist" and conservative movements, such as Jainism and the Mennonites, have often been the most peaceful — the Jains perhaps more than any other group in human history.

Moreover, the politics of violence are unclear. There is the Gandhian problem — what should he say about resistance to Hitler in view of the Holocaust and other mass-murders and acts of gratuitous warfare? Ordered society and civilization seem to imply the use of force. Muslims, always clear on this point, do not apologize for their heroic attempts at building a new civilization under God. Christians have tried a compromise, through the theory of the just war (and revolution); but with nuclear weapons? Can there be a just war here? Or even the slight threat of a nuclear holocaust in order to prevent war? It is not surprising if there is doubt and confusion about how we should frame the whole question of the justification of the use of violence. But as has been noted, we now live in a tightly interwoven world community, and older norms, which date from wider spaces and different times, can no longer be appealed to.

We may note, of course, that it is primarily nationalism which has brought violence into the modern world, though sometimes reinforced by religion or ideology. Aggrandizing nations become imperialist. The period of colonialism was one when countries expanded their interests most nakedly. But worse were the great wars brought about by clashes between nations. (Fascism, incidentally, is simply an ideology of hypernationalism and authoritarianism.. Moreover, since World War II there have been plenty of lesser wars almost invariably sparked by nations aspiring to attain sovereignty and liberation, or to wrest territories from others, usually on an ethnic basis. There have been a few non-ethnic struggles relating to supposed questions of social justice, such as the first J.V.P. uprising in Sri Lanka in 1971, the campaigns of leftists in the Argentine, the insurgency of the Sendero Luminoso in Peru, etc. They are terrible warnings of the misery and futility of leftist-justified violence. But chiefly, as I say, the problems relate to nations and lesser ethnic groups. Religions, which tend to be spiritual transnational corporations, can moderate these conflicts. It is certainly not wise to support those elements within a religion which tend to exacerbate them.

It seems therefore reasonable to suppose that a degree of violence is necessary to maintain order within and between nations. As a result a rigid pacifism is not feasible, so that, paradoxically, strictly harmless people such as Jains become parasitical on the wider order and force of society. Nevertheless we can agree that it is desirable to minimize violence. In a democracy, potential conflicts are settled by the ballot and the parliamentary vote. Those who argue for a new approach to the use of violence, beyond the older notions of just war, *jihad* and the empowerment of *ksatriya,* or warrior class, in traditional Hindu law, therefore have a strong case.

For this reason it is important for followers of different traditions to take a critical attitude to traditions of warfare and
martial religious imagery. Though not entirely blameless
where war is concerned, Buddhism presents itself as the
least warlike, perhaps, of the world's religions, with the
exception of Jainism. But there remain problems for
Buddhists, as with others, in explaining the prevalence of
violence. My view is that a doctrine of the minimization of
violence, if sincerely held, might be the best ethic to follow.
It is a variation on the utilitarianism of happiness. It would
be necessary to judge how far such an intention could be
discerned within a religion if it were to guide the choice
between one tradition or subtradition and another.

The same criterion would apply to individuals, for example
in relation to punishments. Also, the diminution in violent
behaviour is important, especially in relation to people of
unequal power. Because drugs and alcohol may stimulate
violence, at the very least they need to be used in modera-
tion. The concept of diminishing violence should also per-
vade attitudes to sexuality, gender and so on.

This connects with a most vital teaching of Gandhi. You
cannot guarantee non-violence if you have violent feelings.
Hatred of enemies bursts forth naturally as violence. And so
an important part of ethical training relates to the cultivation
of benevolent feelings towards enemies and others you may
dislike. I do not think there is much dispute that the religion
which places most emphasis on this in a clear and practical
way is Buddhism. But there are places where the same kind

of cultivation of love for enemies is found among Jews, Sufis, Christians and many others. But Buddhist methods of meditation explicitly deal with the calming of emotions of hatred and their substitution by benevolence and compassion.

To sum up: there are lessons to be drawn from the use of the criterion of the minimization of violence, which range from the need to damp down the fires of nationalism, to the desirability of meditating in order to improve our characters in relation to feelings of hatred and animosity. As for the injustices which often breed ethnic violence, I shall come to those later in relation to the other criteria.

The criterion of environmental and related issues

As population increases, the globe shrinks. In this context some worldviews show themselves irresponsible. Of course, the whole of our problems cannot be put down to population problems, but to greed and the way capitalist economies are run. But let us begin with population. Here there is no doubt that, empirically, the most effective contraceptive is being bourgeois! As we have noted already, Catholic Italy now (1994) has the lowest birth-rate in the world, despite the Pope's pleas. But the Pope's pleas are themselves open to scrutiny, to put it no more strongly, when his teachings, from the nature of Roman Catholicism as an institution, tend to have most influence in poor nations, such as those of Latin America and parts of Africa. It is becoming doubtful whether the earth will be able to support the rising billions. Moreover, it is to the credit of the modern epoch that we have come (in the West) to take animal rights more seriously, raising a question mark over the mass production of food. Further, justice demands a better distribution of resources. The spread of middle class values has had spectacular results in terms of producing economic miracles in some East Asian and oil-rich Mid-Eastern countries. Perhaps economic miracles will gradually spread throughout the world. But before then we shall have to think about our scale and manner of consumption. Some religious traditions have important lessons here. The monastic and parallel traditions of a number of major spiritual traditions point to more modest ways of living.

Important, too, in this whole evaluation of humanity and its resources is the issue of women's rights, since this affects resources in two ways, as well as being of vital concern in itself. For, given freedom where they do not have it, women are more likely to find education and relief from excess child-bearing, and to develop greater ambitions about the quality rather than the quantity of life. In fact, the realization of justice,both for poorer and ethnically oppressed people will spring from our next criterion. Not surprisingly, people sickened by long oppression will often migrate from one religion to another, as with those untouchables who followed their leader Dr Ambedkar, in leaving traditional Hinduism and becoming Buddhists. But it is often a question of joining a reforming movement within the larger tradition.

The vital nature of toleration

In this sketch of three criteria, a special place must be assigned to toleration. This is of direct relevance to religious traditions. But we can see its relevance to the other criteria by considering briefly the most spectacular ideological failure of our age. Because Marxism was intolerant and despised democracy, only borrowing its forms when it suited, there was no sense of responsibility at the top. Hence the truly horrifying pollutions and environmental disasters which it spawned, throughout Eastern Europe and Siberia (not to mention parts of China). Moreover, it suppressed — or attempted to suppress — traditional religions, from Buddhism to Orthodoxy and from Islam to Judaism. It also, despite its egalitarian ideology, continued the great oppression of women. True feminism was too critical and democratic to be easily allowed by the gerontocracy. Moreover, these features were built into Marx's ideology as interpreted by Lenin.

Now that the whole of the earth's land surface, excepting Antarctica, is covered with nation-states, the question of religious and minority toleration becomes ever more pressing. Older attempts to impose a single law are no longer appropriate. All this means that the demand for modernism in religion is reinforced. The vitality of a liberal ethos is essential if injustice is not to occur.

Toleration also provides the framework of societies which

can debate the truth. It provides the background for productive work in science and the humanities. It is often a dilemma for old established religions as to how far internal or external criticism should be allowed or even encouraged. A tradition has to be transmitted, and this can be facilitated by unquestioning obedience to authority. Nevertheless, the days of such closed societies are virtually over. There is, at the time of writing, some debate in Iran as to whether satellite dishes for television should be permitted. They are already sprouting in Teheran and other cities. It is difficult to suppress them, yet as is well known, they give the user access to the world, in particular to elements of Western culture displeasing to the Islamic values of the Iranian Revolution. The fact is that because of modern technology, it is virtually impossible to isolate any society from wider debate and foreign values. So as we move towards a global civilization, there is bound to be controversy. It is healthier, therefore, to expose religions, like everything else, to the critical gaze. This need not be hostile. Far from it. The treasures of tradition themselves often shine a critical beam on all sorts of modern values. South Asian religions, for instance, have done much to promote the greatly increased awaresss in recent times of animal rights (often neglected in the Christian West).

Let us now move on to a discussion of the question of choice and an ideology for our emerging global civilization.

CHAPTER SIX

JUDGING WORLDVIEWS IN THE GLOBAL WORLD

I have proposed a number of criteria by which to judge worldviews. The major list is as follows: modernism; richness of spiritual experience; openness to other traditions; attractiveness of ritual and scriptural offerings; situational relevance; effectiveness plus the ethical criteria of the minimization of violence; reverence for resources; and the promotion of toleration (which should be thought to include the defence of justice for the oppressed against social, economic and international discrimination).

I shall deal briefly later with the kind of person who might have the courage and motivation to embrace these criteria or welcome their consequences. What kind of saint would display this kind of attitude to religion and religions? And there might be some questions too as to which ideals of salvation and the future life might encourage such sanctity.

There is also the overarching question as to whether there is some worldview which, while preserving the best from the traditions, might yet be appropriate to the new global citizen .

There is an attraction here in what might be thought of as the intermediate religions — those lying between the particularities of the values of small-scale societies and the universalisms of the great religions. I am thinking above all of Judaism but also of the religions of the Parsees, the Sikhs, the Taoists, and so on. Generally these religions do not seek any vast missionary expansion: they see themselves as contributing to a wider civilization and ultimately to the global community. Perhaps the bigger faiths — Christianity, Islam, Buddhism, Hinduism and Confucianism — need to see themselves in the same light. For the fact is that reflection will show them that they will remain, in the distantly foreseeable future, as minorities. So will scientific humanism, despite its often smug assumption that humans will come to accept a 'rational' outlook in due course. As minorities, perhaps these worldviews may recognize the need for some theory which will make sense of a peaceful *modus vivendi* with their rivals.

Towards a global ideology

Because of the great variation of religions and, more generally, worldviews, and because of the fact that some major worldviews do not have a divine Creator figure — notably Jainism and Theravada Buddhism — it is hard to accept the otherwise attractive philosophy of (for example) Swami Vivekananda and John Hick. This is a pluralism which says that all religions really point to the same truth, a Divine Reality beyond the various images and doctrinal formulations of the diverse faiths. This Reality is like the Sun, around which revolve the planetary religions. Such a "Copernican" revolution attracts people, since it provides a simple solution to the various shapes of the diverse traditions.

There are Westerners and others who might think that this attention to traditional religions is ridiculous — that they are all false, products of a bygone age of human knowledge. But they do not go away; and a humanist prejudice seems to me no better than any other kind. Some Christians likewise dismiss all other worldviews as creations of the Devil, or as idolatrous. No: if we are to try and evolve a global ideology, then it needs to recognize religions as well as secular worldviews.

The key may lie in some dialectical formulation. I shall come to this in a moment; but let me first comment upon ethnicity and nationalism. While nations, can of course, be a menace to one another, they can also live amicably together, substituting football matches for warfare. But even so, other problems remain — for example all those peoples such as the Kurds who are prevented from attaining sovereignty, or if not that, at least some enriching autonomy. The nation which is suppressed becomes more violent in its demands. While the division of people into nation-states is not perhaps the best ultimate goal, this is necessary in effect, in order to be able to go beyond. It is better to be given autonomy or independence than to burn with frustration. So we may in due course need to look to a new and even more complex world order. But apart from this application of cultural justice, we need also to see a levelling of wealth in the world, so that at least the sharp injustice of our present economic maldistribution is mitigated. The half-starved children of Central Africa will soon be gazing at the well-nourished casts of American sitcoms; and the dusty offspring of untouchables will be fascinated by the gyrations of rich Europeans. These are some of the ingredients of social explosion. Both in self-interest and in recognition of the rights of all human beings, the richer world will have to promote new wealth among the poor.

But we still have the dilemma of what to do about rival and different religions. Naturally neither Parsees or Jews want to be assimilated into some other faith, nor Christians inhibited from proclaiming their message; even Buddhists, who are very modest, though effective; missionaries do not want to be stopped from spreading their message of enlightenment. Much has to do with methods: it is obvious here that religions have to eschew the use of force and to rely simply upon persuasion and preaching. There can surely be nothing wrong with such peaceful self-selling. In a new global order it would have to be accompanied by respect for others. Loving one's enemies would clearly include loving both those who have different notions of the ultimate and different customs.

It seems to me that a framework for such friendly rivalry might be a kind of theory of complementarity. The heart of this would be the thought that religions and worldviews are dialectically related to one another. They present divergent lifestyles and values as well as theories of the human condition, not to mention paths of spirituality and emphases of religious experience. But they can learn from one another and so by implication modify one another as time goes by. Who knows what will emerge out of the dialectic of world values? Moreover, apart from their spiritual values they can share cultural riches, such as the variety of music and literature both of the past and of the emerging present. So the future of religions lies in a dialogue, in which different adherents will be asked neither to give up nor to compromise their deeper values. But they can still hold to the complementarity hypothesis as the framework for a specific global ideology.

Now I do not for a minute suppose that such a position will prevent radicals from taking other positions. A worldview will not prevent bombings, but it may be one of the conditions which helps to damp down violence and prejudice.

Underpinning the Complementarity Worldview are various thoughts. One is that diversity is itself a richness in the global civilization. Another is the thesis that in the long run, truth is something which emerges dialectically, by open competition between different ways of formulating it. Third, that peaceful persuasion, through example and argument, rather than violent confrontation, is natural to the global order. It may be that we would have to be coercive in relation to those who try to coerce. But peaceful methods remain the world's crying need.

The Complementarity Worldview would not preclude people from subscribing to different worldviews among themselves: it would be a kind of Meta-Worldview. It could act as an adjunct to one's primary religious or other commitment. No doubt it would be necessary to interpret Complementarism through drawing on elements in one's own tradition. For instance, the Christian might say that all faiths derive some inspiration from God, and that God favours the richness and variety of the world's spirituality, so that each tradition could help the others to remain honest. Too much power in any one tradition is corrupting.

Religions change. In their future evolution religions may converge. That is not for us to foresee at present. It could be that by undergoing changes as a result of the dialectic of global civilization, Vivekananda may eventually be proved right. But, as I say, it is not something to prophesy. The world I do foresee is one that retains considerable differences of ideas and customs. Within the interstices between worldviews many new faiths will continue to arise, often eclectically. Perhaps with a Complementarist vision they can learn to work together.

The global citizen and her spirituality

What virtues should be bred in the global citizen? She should be sage (taking some benefit from Confucianism), since she should if possible recognize the divergent traditions of the world. Education is and will remain highly relevant; as is the need for education to include at least something on the religions of the globe. She should not be indifferent to the large patterns of human religious experience: she should be both a yogi and a devotee, if at least she finds the gods to inspire *bhakti,* or devotion. She will probably be loyal to a given tradition and, if so, should practise it with fervour and yet with a degree of modernism and self-criticism. She should be tolerant, and self-confident about her own tradition, as interpreted according to a modernist or liberal ethos. She should love and be benevolent towards all living creatures, but especially humans and in particular enemies. She should induce in herself positive attitudes which will breed toleration. She should have profound equanimity, for the challenges of today's world are both complex and biting. All this should go with such other virtues as arise from different aspects of our human nature — as for example the powerful urgings of sexuality, which need to be channelled and calmed, since they are a potent cause of violence. All these virtues need to be worked out amid the vagaries of family relationships, work, community and the shifting world. It is a noble and difficult vision.

What is salvation for such a person? What is true happiness? I think it could simply be satisfaction in doing one's best for our community of ultimate concern, namely humanity as a whole and to a lesser degree the living world about us. Or it could, according to some scenarios, be found in a heavenly closeness to the Divine. Or it might be found in the prospect of continued ascent up the ladder of rebirth (I say continued ascent, because it is normally held to be a precious treasure to be born human, and we might hope, in a future, for further "promotion").

Indeed, the question of the nature of our life — whether we are subject to rebirth, or whether we simply die, or whether we go beyond death to the possibilities of heavenly or hellish life — is one that will exercise our model person. Will she argue that reincarnation gives us a more tolerant attitude, because the question of salvation is not so urgent, and so preaching need not be so shrill? Or will she cleave to the heaven-oriented theistic traditions of the West?

I am not in this small book answering these particular questions. I am only providing a framework for your consideration of the large issues which are bound to arise when religions come together. Of one thing I am certain — and that is that the riches of the varied worldviews are great. It has been cynically said that comparative religion makes you comparatively religious. My experience and observation has been the opposite. The exploration of the world's faiths, from Native American to East Asian religions, from Judaism to Zulu Zionism, from Scientific Humanism to Eastern Orthodoxy and from Islam to Methodism leaves me, the explorer, more deeply affected, not less. But baffled? Well, somewhat: it is important for humans to recognize the many potent questions that remain puzzling and unanswered. But bafflement is the fuel of exploration —exploration of the staggering human heritage of spiritual life which deepens your soul.

This is to say nothing of the myths of modern literature and the profundities of the world's diverse heritage of music. But they all point to the lesson that happiness and sorrow should be deep and transforming experiences. You may complain that this small book contains few answers. Well, to that I reply: it is for you to try to answer the questions that only you can raise.

My plea above all, though, is for peace between ideologies and religions. It is surprising what cruelties humans are capable of when they think themselves justified by some Cause. But it is a tranquil thing to read a book, and so I hope I have helped a little with your thinking.

Brief Bibliography

Cromwell Crawford, S. (ed.)(1939) *World Religions and Global Ethics* .
Hick, John (1985) *Problems of Religious Pluralism* .
Hick, John (1989) *An Interpretation of Religion* .
Kellenberger, J. (1993) *Inter-Religious Models and Criteria.*
Otto, Rudolf, (1923) *The Idea of the Holy*
Sharma, Arvind (ed.) (1993) *God, Truth and Reality.*
Smart, Ninian (1960) *A Dialogue of Religions.*
Smart, Ninian (1989) *The World's Religions.*
Stace, W.T. (1960) *Mysticism and Philosophy.*
Swami Vivekananda (1964) *The Complete Works.*
Thakur, Shivesh (1980) *Religion and Rational Choice.*
Underhill, Evelyn (1911) *Mysticism.*
Zaehner, R.C. (1957) *Mysticism Sacred and Profane.*

INDEX

Abraham, 31
Africa: 19, 22, 40, 41; independent churches in, 23
Aga Khan, 32
Ahimsa, 34, 35
Ahmadiya, 31
Alawi, 31
Allah, 50
Ambedkar, Dr, 96
America, North, 19, 24
Amida Buddha, 33, 40
Amitabha, 33, 49, 53
Anabaptists, 18, 77, *see also* Mennonites
Analects, the, 53
Anglicans, 18, 30
Animal Rights, 27, 98, *see also* Bionism
Argentina, 93
Aristotle, 81
Arjuna, 46
Australia, 23, 40
Avalukitesvara, 49

Avatara, 49
Ayatollahs, 64

Baptists, 18
Benares, 51
Bhagavadgita, the, 36, 49
Bhakti, 35, 36, 105
Bhedabhedavada, 54
Bible, the, 11, 13, 41, 46, 70
Bionism, 27
Birth control, 88
Bodh-Gaya, 52
Bodhisattva, 33, 34, 49
Brahmins, 33, 36, 78
Buddha, Amida, *see* Amida Buddha
Buddha, The, (Gautama), 17, 19, 34, 38, 45, 52, 53
Buddhas: celestial, 13, 33, 34; earthly, 49
Buddhism: effect on Far East, 4; general, 9, 24, 33, 35, 37, 38, 39, 43, 47, 48, 58, 62, 69, 74, 80, 81, 90, 94, 95, 100; in Japan, 40; myth, 49; Sangha,

17, 34, 63; sexism, 88; and
Untouchables, 96; *see also* Amida
Buddha; Bodhisattva; Buddha, The;
Buddhas; Chinese Buddhism;
Meditation Buddhism; Mahayana
Buddhism; Nichiren Buddhism; Pure
Land Buddhism; Tantric Buddhism;
Theravada Buddhism; Zen Buddhism
Buddhist–Jewish dialogue, 2
Buddhists, Tibetan, 24
Burma, 19
Burundi, 87

Caliph, 32
Caliphate, 32
Calvinists, 18, 72–3
Cambodia, 19
Capitalism, 57–8
Carter, Jimmy, 3
Catholics: 17; Croats, 3
Catholicism: 23, 30—31, 64, 72—73,
77; structure, 30; Zen, 2; *see also*
Roman Catholicism
Chile, 57
Chinese Buddhism, 24, 40, 43
China, 20, 23, 37, 49
Christ: 42, 50, 52, 53, 74, 75, 78;
proof of divinity, 13, 14; teaching of
love, 17
Christian Science, 18
Christianity: 22ff., 42ff., 53, 58, 60,
66, 74, 78, 90, 92, 100, 101; central
tenets, 30; denominational choice, 2;
division of East and West, 30; doctri-
nal content, 16–17, 18, 29–30, 52;

Eucharist, 17, 52; Gospel, 69; and
Neoplatonism, 44; and sexuality, 88;
doctrine of Trinity, 16, 17, 29, 30
Christian Yoga, 2
Chu Hsi, 37
Church of Scotland, 64
Church, The: ideological divisions,
19; sects, 16, 17, 30; success of, 4
Colonialism, 92
Comparative religion, practice of, 9
Comparative Religion, Museum of,
(Glasgow), 4–5
Comte, August, 82
Confucianism, 22, 37–8, 39, 58, 59,
74, 88, 90, 100, 105
Confucius, 37, 75
Congregationalists, 18
Contemplation, *see* Mysticism
Cosmological Argument, 83–4
Croats, 3

Devil, the, 101
Dharma, 39, 88
Diamond Vehicle, *see* Vajtayana
Druze, 31
Dukes of Chou, 49

Eliot, 43
Enlightenment, the, European, 27,
28, 56
Ethics, 48–49, 62, 72, 81, 85, 88,
89ff., 94
Ethnicity, 101–2
Eucharist, the, 17, 52
Evil, problem of, 89

Faith: absence of and worldview, 2; balance, importance of in understanding, 16ff.; certainty and certitude in, 11–12; essentials of, 74–5; objectivity, 5; nature of True Faith, 5; personal values in choosing, 60, 84
Fascism, 83, 93
Feuerbach, Ludwig, 65, 66, 82
French Revolution, 82
Freud, 65, 66
Fruits of spiritual and scriptural injunctions, 71–2, 80, 84, 86ff.
Fundamentalism: 59, 69, 70, 76; American, 59

Ghandi, 20, 92, 94
Global Citizen, the: spirituality and virtues, 105; and salvation, 106
Global ideology, *see* Ideology, global
God: 46, 47, 52, 67, 68, 78, 83, 92, 104; proof of existence, 12–13; guidance of, 90; response to prayer, 17; transcendence of, 90
Gospel, the, 69
Graeco–Roman philosophy, 22
Granth Sahib, 37
Great Vehicle, *see* Mahayana Buddhism
Greek Orthodoxy, 24
Guru Granth, 69, 70
Gurus, the, 37

Hadith, 31
Hasidism, 54

Hebrew scriptures, 69, 70
Hegel, 66
Hegelianism, 65
Hick, John, 5, 101
Hinayana Buddhism, see Theravada Buddhism
Hinduism, 2, 20, 22, 33, 35, 36, 44ff., 49, 55ff., 64, 69, 70, 78, 88, 93, 100
Hindus, 24
Hitler, Adolf, 8, 62, 92
Holocaust, the, 23–4, 29, 92
Holy, Idea of the, (Otto), 45
Holy Sepulchre, 51, 52
Holy, The, 44, 45
Humanism, 101
Humanness, *see Jen*
Huxley, Aldous, 5

Idea of the Holy, (Otto), 45
Ideology, global, 101ff.
Ideologies, secular, 80ff.
India, 19, 20, 36
Individualism, 27, 28, 56–7, 59–9, 60–1, 77
Indonesia, 23
IranianRevolution, 98
Islam: 22ff., 72ff., 80, 88, 92, 98, 100, 107; doctrine, 31–2; ethics, 31–2; modernism, 2–3; global Muslim population, 23; origins, 31; organization, 32; sects, 31; spread of, 31; *see also* Qur'an
Isaiah, 49
Isma'ili, 31
Isonzo, the, 45

Israel: 24; history, 78; State of, formation, 29
Italy, Catholic, 76, 95

Jainism: 12, 22, 27, 34–5, 48, 92ff., 101; organization of, 35
Japan: 53, 59; Buddhism in, 40; Emperor, divinity of, 59; Meiji Era, 59
Jen, 39
Jerusalem, 51
Jews: 10, 49, 54, 79; persecution of, 28; *see also* Judaism
Jihad, 93
Job, Biblical, 46
Judaism: 10–11, 22, 23–4, 74, 88, 90, 100, 107; Talmud, 28; doctrine, 29; movements in, 28–9; razing of Temple, 4
Judging faiths, 7ff.

Kabbalism, 29, 43, 54
Kali, 35, 49
Kant, 27
Karma, 36, 47–8
Korea, 23, 40, 57
Krishna, 25, 52, 53, 73, 78
Ksatriya, 93
K'ung, *see* Confucius
Kurds, 102

Laos, 19
Lao-tsu, 38, 49, 52
Lenin, 97
Liberal economics, success and

failure of, 14–15
Liberation Theeology, 60
Lesser Vehicle, *see* Theravada Buddhism
Li, 39
Lotus Sutra, 40
Love for enemies, 94–5, 103
Luther, 53
Lutherans, 18, 30

Maddonas, 55
Mahabarata, 36
Mahavira, 34, 35
Mahayana, the, 49
Mahayana Buddhism, 22, 23, 33, 42, 53, 77
Malaysia, 23
Maoism, 26
Mao Zedong, 38
Marx, 65, 66, 97
Marxism: 26ff., 57ff., 66, 81, 82, 97; in China, 20; failures, 15
Meditation Buddhism, 38
Mecca, 51, 52
Meiji Era, Japan, 59
Mencius, 90
Mennonites, 92, *see also* Anabapists
Merton, Thomas, 53
Methodism, 107
Middle class, global spread of values, 96; *see also* Values
Middle East, 22, 47
Modernism, 19, 70–1, 80, 81, 84, 85, 97
Monasticism, 30

Moral Training, 63
Mormonism, 18
Mormons, 24, 25
Moses, 52
Moses and Monotheism, (Freud), 66
Mughals, 36–7
Muhammad, 31, 50, 52, 73ff.
Museum of Comparative Religion,
Glasgow, 4–5
Muslim Brotherhood, 32
Muslims: 13, 23, 24, 45, 48; born-
again, 59
Mysterium tremendum et fascinans,
44, 45
Mysticism: 67, 73, 81, in
Christianity, 53; impersonal aspect
of, 43–4; similarities, 43ff.
Myths: 50; African, 90; creation, 90

Nationalism: 14, 25–6, 28, 81, 82–3,
95, 101–2, effects on religious
denomination espoused, 19; and vio-
lence, 92, 93; Indian subcontinental,
36; relation to religion, 3
Nation–States: 102; idea of, 25
Neoconfucianism, 37–8, 39, 54
Neoplatonism, 44
New Age, 25
New religious movements, 24–5
New Zealand, 23
Nichiren Buddhism, 40
Nirvana, 17, 68, 90
Nuclear weapons, 92
Numinous, the, encounter with, 67,
73

Old Testament, Biblical, 46
One Reality, concept of, 55
Openness to other traditions, 74, 80
Original Sin, 90
Orthodoxy: 18; structure, 30
Other person, the, empathy with, 7–8
'Otherness', holy sense of, 45ff.
Otto, Rudolf, 43, 44, 45, 46

Pacific region, 19, 23
Panama Canal treaties, 3
Papacy, the, 30
Parsees, 24, 32, 64, 100, *see also*
Zoroastrianism
Personal circumstances, importance
of, 75ff., 80
Peru, 93
Philippines, the, 23
Pilgrimage, 51
Pope John XXIII, 75
Pope, the, 95, *see also* Papacy, the
Population problem, 95ff.
Projection theories, 66
Protestantism, 23, 27, 30, 56, 58, 75,
77
Protestants, 18
Pure Land Buddhism, 40

Quakers, 17, 18, 88
Qur'an, (Koran), 13, 31, 53, 69, 70

Rama, 52, 73, 78
Ramanuja, 75
Ramayana, 36

Rationality, 83ff.
Reality, Divine, the, 101
Reformation, the, 18, 30, 73
Reflection on values, fruits of, 10ff.
Refracted theism, 55, 56
Reincarnation, 39, 47–8, 59
Religion: dimensions of, definition, 16ff.; future change in, 21
Religions: extent of agreement 5–6, 103ff.; blending with value systems, 3, 4; common ground in, 42ff.; dimensions of, 16ff.; evolution and future of, 104–5; intermediate-size, 100; major, effect of industrialism and colonialism on, 19–20; minor, 54–5; and nationalism, 3; important world regions, 22ff.; self-proving, 14; transcendental unity of, 51; nature of the Ultimate, 6; *see also* Faith
Religious dialogue, 103
Religious experience, 65, 67, 80
Resources, global, 87–8, 89
Rhadakrishnan, 20, 36
Rituals, 51, 77ff., 80
Roman Catholicism: 18, 55, 75–6, 89, 95; Vatican II, 75, 76
Roman Empire, 4, 23
Russia, 24
Rwanda, 87

Sabbath, Jewish, 8
Sacrifice, 78, 91
Salvation, 17
Sangha, the, 17, 34, 63

Santeria, 41
Sarnath, 52
Scandinavia, and social democracy, 58
Scientific Humanism, 27, 28, 80ff., 100, 107
Scripture, interpretation of, 3
Secular worldviews, 25
Sendero Luminoso, 93
Serbs Orthodox, 3
Sexism, 57
Sexuality, 88, 94, 105
Shamanism, 23
Shinran, 40, 53
Shinto, 22
Shiva, 35, 49
Siberia, 25
Sikhism, 22, 36–7, 54, 59, 69, 100
Sikhs, 24
Sinhalese, Buddhists, 3
Sita, 78
Smart, 43
Smrti, 70
South Asia, 22
Sovereignty, 102
Soviet Empire: 12, 26; collapse of, 12
Sri Lanka: 4, 17, 19, 22, 33, 43; JVP uprising, 93
Sri Lankan Buddhism, 43, *see also* Theravada Buddhism
St John of the Cross, 43
Stace, 43
St Paul, 46
Sufis, 32

Sufism, 44, 54, 63, 73ff.
Syadvada, 12
Syncretism, 3

Talmud, 28
Tamils: 77; Hindu, 2
Tantric Buddhism, 33
Tao 38, 39
Taoism: 22, 38, 49, 69, 74, 100; organization, 39
Tao-te Ching, 38
Teachers, judging of, 62ff.
Ten Commandments, 16–17
Theravada Buddhism, 17, 22, 33, 34, 43, 44, 46, 58, 64, 72, 77, 101
Tibetan Buddhists, 74
Toleration, 14, 15, 89, 97ff.
Torah, 28
Trinity, Holy: 16, 17,30; doctrine of, 29
Truth, 62–3, 64, 68, 70, 71, 79, 98
Turks, 24

Ultimate, the: nature of from common ground of religions, 6
Underhill, 43
Unificationists, 25
Unitarians, 18
United Nations, 87
Untouchables, and acceptance of Buddhism, 96
Upanishads, 36
Utalitarianism in modern philosophical traditions, 91

Vajtayana, 34
Vatican II, 75, 76
Veda, 69
Vendanta, 36, 55
Vietnam: 19, 23; and USA, 92
Violence: 87, 89, 91ff., 103, 105; minimization of, 94, 95; politics of, 92
Virgin of Guadalupe, 55
Virgin, the, legends about, 55
Vishnu, 35, 49, 50
Vivekananda, 5, 10, 35, 36, 50, 52, 101, 104
Voodoo, 41

Wailing Wall, 51
Wang Yangming, 54
Women's rights, 96, 97
World's Parliament of Religion, Chicago, 1893, 50

Xavier, Francis, 53

Yin and Yang, 38
Yogis, 43, 73
Yorubas, 24

Zachner, 43
Zen Buddhism, 40
Zen Catholicism, 2
Zionism, 29
Zoroastrianism, 22, 32–3
Zoroastrians, 24, *see also* Parsees

Also available in the *Briefings* Series

BEFORE THE BEGINNING is a radical attempt to explain and rede-
fine the origins and purpose of creation. Professor Ellis deals
clearly and authoritatively with new scientific theories explaining
how things began and elucidates the laws which control the opera-
tion of the universe. In addition, he describes the complex mecha-
nism by which the laws of physics appear to govern and facilitate,
as well as to sustain human life. His conclusions about the very
meaning of life are often unexpected, but the process by which he
reaches them is illuminating and scientifically sound, as would be
expected from one of the world's foremost cosmologists.

George Ellis is Professor of Cosmic Physics at SISSA in Trieste,
Italy and Professor of Applied Mathematics at the University of
Cape Town, South Africa. A former Fellow of Peterhouse,
Cambridge, he is GC Macvittie Visiting Professor of Astronomy
in the School of Mathematics at Queen Mary and Westfield
College, London University. Amongst his many publications, he is
the author, jointly with Stephen Hawking, of *The Large Scale
Structure of Space-Time*.

'Ellis is an eminent cosmologist and mathematical physicist who
has contributed significantly to present-day understanding of the
nature of the beginning of the universe. ..Ellis devotes the first two
thirds of the book to developing the reader's understanding of the
scientific issues. He does this with prose that is consise and accu-
rate....He is most concerned with the question of why life exists ...
the discussion of this issue is very good.....Recommended.'
CHOICE

IDEOLOGY AFTER THE FALL OF COMMUNISM looks at the likely developments in ideological thinking after the fall of the Berlin Wall in 1989. Will one particular brand of political philosophy come to dominate world thinking now that Soviet Communism is no longer a force to be reckoned with? If so, will it be liberal democracy - the system prevailing in the USA and the EEC? Or will some other kind of irresistible movement sweep all before it - nationalism, religious fundamentalism, market forces raw in tooth and claw, or some form of non-Marxian socialism? The author explores all these possibilities and offers his own bold and controversial predictions.

Peter Collins - Editor of *Briefings* - gained first class honours in Philosophy at London University. He now teaches Political Philosophy in the University of Cape Town's Department of Political Studies, where he is presently Senior Lecturer.

'This remarkable short book of a new series to explain complex issues will bea valuable tool in teaching introductory college courses in politics and ideology... A great little paperback suitable for graduate and undergraduate students as well as the interested public.' *CHOICE*

GENOCIDE— THE PSYCHOLOGY OF MASS MURDER
This book attempts to make sense of the senseless. Its author considers cases of genocide past and present. He shows how various factors - political, economic, military and other - combine to produce the explosive mixture of circumstances in which genocide becomes possible. Tragically timely, the book demonstrates how contemporary events in Yugoslavia and elsewhere might have been foreseen and prevented.

Peter du Preez is Professor of Psychology at the University of Cape Town where he has concentrated on the uses of psychology to explain social and historical trends and the strategies of political debate. Professor du Preez is the author of *Dangerous Connections* (Buren, 1974), *The Politics of Identity* (Blackwell, 1980) and *A Science of Mind* (Academic Press, 1991), of which the journal *Contemporary Review* wrote:

'This incisive, witty and sophisticated work combines much of what is good in current philosophy of science with much of what is good in the new history of psychology.'